NEUROLOGICAL EVALUATION OF THE PSYCHOGENIC PATIENT

Editors:
W. Lynn Smith, Ph.D.
Dept. of Biological Sciences
University of Denver
Denver, Colorado

Michael H. Hitchcock, M.D.
Neurosensory Diagnostic Center
Swedish Medical Center
Englewood, Colorado

Lavar G. Best, Ph.D.
Swedish Medical Center
Porter Memorial Hospital
Denver, Colorado

SP MEDICAL & SCIENTIFIC BOOKS
a division of Spectrum Publications, Inc.
New York • London

SPECTRUM PUBLICATIONS, INC.
175-20 Wexford Terrace, Jamaica, N.Y. 11432

Library of Congress Cataloging in Publication Data
Main entry under title:

Neurological evaluation of the psychogenic patient.

Includes index.
1. Medicine, Psychosomatic. I. Smith, W. Lynn (Wallace Lynn), 1922-   . II. Hitchcock, Michael H. III. Best, Lavar. (DNLM: 1. Diagnosis, Differential. 2. Neurologic examination. 3. Psychophysiologic disorders.   WM 90 P962]
RC49.P65   616.08   81-8570
ISBN 0-89335-147-7   AACR2

CONTRIBUTORS

Lavar G. Best, Ph.D.
Neurosensory Diagnostic Center
Swedish Medical Center
Englewood, Colorado

Donald L. Duerksen, B.A.
Cortical Function Laboratories
Porter Memorial Hospital
Denver, Colorado

Michael H. Hitchcock, M.D.
Swedish Medical Center
Porter Memorial Hospital
Denver, Colorado

Brien P. James, M.D.
Swedish Medical Center
Porter Memorial Hospital
Denver, Colorado

H. Merskey, D.M., F.R.C.P. (C),
 F.R.C. Psych.
Department of Psychiatry
University of Western Ontario
and
London Psychiatric Hospital
London, Ontario

Will P. Pirkey, M.D.
Swedish Medical Center
Porter Memorial Hospital
Denver, Colorado

Richard W. Rewey, M.D.
Swedish Medical Center
Porter Memorial Hospital
Denver, Colorado

Charles E. Seibert, M.D.
Swedish Medical Center
Porter Memorial Hospital
Denver, Colorado

W. Lynn Smith, Ph.D.
Cortical Function Laboratories
Porter Memorial Hospital
Denver, Colorado
and
White Memorial Medical Center
Los Angeles, California
and
Department of Biological Sciences
University of Denver
Denver, Colorado

Gary D. Vander Ark, M.D.
Swedish Medical Center
Porter Memorial Hospital
Denver, Colorado

CONTENTS

Introduction

INTRODUCTION

Througout the centuries, medicine has been ever-changing. In the Middle Ages, medicine as a field of study was forced into the constraints of philosophy and theology. Medical knowledge was not based on careful observation and experimentation, but rather on non-critical acceptance of the classic teachings of the ancient masters such as Hippocrates and Galen. Diseases were tied to demons and impurities of living; miracle cures and mysticism surrounded medicine in that day. With the coming of the Renaissance in science and the arts, medicine began to develop as a science with the formation of medical schools such as those at Salerno, Montpellier and Bologna. The careful anatomical dissections and descriptions of Leonardo de Vinci and, later, Andreas Versalius led to the modern concept of anatomy. During the seventeenth and eighteenth centuries, physiology, pathology and physical diagnosis were firmly established as fields of study in medicine. Lister, Pasteur, Erlich, Billroth, Osler, Halsted, Virchow and a host of other great men of medicine added to our fund of knowledge in modern medicine. The philosophy of medicine has changed from myth and magic to the view that all diseases have understandable organic causes. In the late nineteenth and early twentieth centuries, there were a few voices in the wilderness such as Freud, Jung, Janet and others who explored the modern demons within our psyche and their relationships to disease. These two rather different directions in medicine have, over this century, developed simultaneously, but more or less in parallel, isolated from one another. Beginning medical students are provided with a physical framework for their understanding of diseases. This physical perspective of disease is continued through the students' clinical clerkship where they are taught to match symptoms and physical signs to particular diseases. This perspective is carried through in the years after formal training in the practice of medicine. Little attention is paid to the psychological reaction of the patient to his disease or injury, let alone to the possible psychogenic causes of many apparent physical signs and symptoms. Likewise, in the psychiatric fields, the training in medicine and neurology are, in many cases, considered to be of secondary importance to the understanding of psychodynamics. The saying, "If all you have is a hammer, everything looks like a nail", is unfortunately all too true in medicine today. Treatment is often determined by one's perception or prejudices about the disease process involved.

In this guidebook, we will attempt to look at the problem patient, that is, the patient with some mixture of organic disease or injury and with significant psychological reactions to their disease or injury. We will attempt to bridge the chasm between purely organic and purely psychological viewpoints on the problem so we may better evaluate, understand and treat such patients. Hundreds of millions of dollars are spent each year in this country on unnecessary tests and procedures, drugs and unwarranted compensation, legal fees, court costs and inapproriate legal settlements because the medical profession does not appreciate and properly deal with the psychological aspects of the organic disease or injury. More important than the costs involved, hundreds of thousands of patients each year undergo the risks of unnecessary drugs, tests and surgical procedures and suffer continued disability because the problem is not properly identified and proper treatment is delayed.

In this publication, we will use the general term, psychogenic disorder, to mean any injury or disease which, to a large extent, has psychologic origins. These disorders are often encountered in general medical practices and may have a superficial appearance of or be derived from real organic ailments or injuries. Herein lies the trap for the physician who does not appreciate the extent of underlying psychological origins of the disorder. Other terms such as hysteria, conversion reaction, functional overlay and malingering may be used in subsequent chapters to denote specific aspects or types of psychogenic disorders.

This guidebook has been written not only for the specialist in psychiatry and the neurosciences, but more importantly for the physician in training and general practitioner who are in the front lines of modern medicine and who are the first to evaluate and guide these patients in the proper direction to alleviate their problems quickly and efficiently. The format will be kept simple and understandable and will deal with only the more common psychogenic disorders rather than being an all-inclusive treatise. This publication has been a combined effort of many specialists within psychiatry and the neurosciences. Each specialist will review one aspect of the evaluation and treatment of the psychogenic patient pertaining to his respective field. Included will be a general discussion of the psychodynamics involved in these problems and some of the treatment modalities which may benefit these patients.

Today, these are indeed problem patients not responsive to the conventional modes of treatment. The problem, however, may not lie so much with the patient as it does with the doctor's perception of the problem. If physicians do not have the proper tools to evaluate and treat these patients, they will be unsuccessful. We authors hope that this guidebook will equip the general medical practitioner as well as his colleagues in the psychiatric and neurological fields with a better understanding of how properly to evaluate these patients and separate them from the typical patients with organic disease so that psychogenic patients may be treated more appropriately.

W. Lynn Smith, Ph.D.
Michael H. Hitchcock, M.D.
LaVar G. Best, Ph.D.

1
The Neurological Examination: Mind Over Matter

MICHAEL H. HITCHCOCK
GARY D. VANDER ARK

The purpose of this volume is to assist the intern, resident, family practitioner or specialist in the neurosciences in the evaluation and treatment of patients with a psychogenic component to their disorder. It is well recognized and appreciated that all patients suffering from an illness or disability have a psychological response to their illness; however, we will consider here those patients whose psychological response to their illness is pathologic in nature and either causes the disability or seriously hinders the improvement of the disability, even with adequate treatment. We will define and discuss three general types of psychogenic patients: the hysteric, the malingerer and the patient with a functional disorder or functional overlay.

True hysteria is rather an uncommon occurrance in a typical medical practice, but recognition of this patient is of utmost importance so that unnecessary tests and procedures can be avoided. This patient does not suffer from any known organic illness, but rather suffers from a disability seen as the unconscious solution, albeit inadequate, to a psychological conflict. The disability may mimic a trauma or a real organic disorder either witnessed or experienced by the patient; however, there may be a temporal separation between the initial trauma or organic disease and the resulting hysterical dysfunction. It represents the unconscious transfer of a psychic conflict to a somatic disorder. There are certain characteristic differences between the hysterical symptoms and the organic disease it mimics and these will be brought out later in the chapter.

The second type of patient, the malingering patient, is also quite rare in the average clinical practice. These patients consciously feign illness or disability to obtain real or imagined secondary gains such as monetary compensation, sympathy from others or revenge for perceived injustices they have suffered. They attempt to deceive others, but they are not deceived themselves. The diagnosis of malingering is a difficult one to make with certainty unless the patient takes you in his confidence and tells you he has fooled you or that the feigned disorder and secondary gains are so obvious that you can confront the patient with confidence and discuss it openly.

The third type, the functional patient or patient with functional overlay, is the largest group of psychogenic patient seen in a medical practice. The terms functional patient and patient with functional overlay are inadequate, but they hold a generally accepted meaning to most of the medical community and therefore will be used. These patients have suffered from some trauma or have a real organic disorder but their symptoms far exceed in both duration and extent the symptoms expected for their particular illness. These patients encompass some of the aspects of hysteria and of malingering, but also show some characteristics that make them unique. Like the malingerer, these patients have suffered from some injury or real organic disorder and often there appears to be a secondary gain involved in the perpetuation of their symptoms; however, like the hysteric, the motivation behind their symptoms may be unconscious to a great extent and the secondary gains may be more vague than simply monetary rewards. Their symptoms may be viewed as an inadequate solution to a personal conflict, as a means of recognition or sympathy or simply a temporary escape from the pressures of life. These patients are somehow unable to cope with the frustrations of life or career and use their symptoms unconsciously to retreat and regroup before embarking on their struggle through life. Some form of depression is not uncommon with the functional patient.

Although a thorough history and neurologic examination and occasionally a few pertinent tests will usually differentiate the psychogenic patient from those with true organic disease or disability, it is sometimes hard to differentiate between the three gorups of psychogenic patients (Miller, 1966). One important point made by Weintraub in his excellent monograph on the subject (Weintraub, 1977) is that the diagnosis of hysteria, and we might add malingering and functional overlay, is not one of exclusion, but rather a diagnosis based on positive evidence of the presence or exaggeration of signs and symptoms which do not appear in any known organic disease. Too often these patients undergo repeated medical workups, costly tests and have been treated with many forms of treatment regimes including surgery which is costly to the patient and society and hold some risk for the patient before the problem is appreciated. These tests and procedures delay the proper diagnosis and treatment of these patients and may reinforce the symptoms by making them seem more legitimate. However, the other side of the argument must be appreciated, that even psychogenic patients die from organic disease. One organic symptom or sign outweighs all other functional or hysterical symptoms. Careful and complete examinations must be performed on all these patients and the physician must estimate the amount of organic disease and the amount of psychogenic component to their illness before he can adequately determine the proper treatment.

HISTORY

The history may give some clue as to the motivation of the patient and also may hold some characteristics that will help you differentiate between the three types of psychogenic patients. The hysterical patient is commonly a rather young attractive female who coyly describes her symptoms in rather vivid terms, as a bolt of lightning, or stabbing or burning pains like red hot rivets. These vivid symptoms are sometimes reported in certain organic disorders but are much more common, often are multiple, and more vividly described in the hysterical patient. These patients probably have been seen by other competent doctors, all of whom have been unable to explain the symptoms to the patient's satisfaction and they have had several tests and/or operative procedures before entering your office. Chadoff describes the hysterical patient as being egocentric, emotionally labile, shallow, tending towards exhibitionism and sexual frigidity (Chadoff, 1974). Pierre Janet coined the phrase, "la belle indifference" for the characteristic way in which the hysterical patient describes his symptoms. There is an apparent lack of concern over rather profound and vividly described bodily dysfunction. Janet also describes a retraction in the field of consciousness in the hysterical patient which leads to absentmindedness and decreased memory (Janet, 1924). These patients seem to suspend critical evaluations and reality testing as an unconscious attempt to retain their hysterical symptoms. Characteristically, the hysterical patient describes many seemingly unrelated symptoms not found in any known syndrome complex of an organic disease. There tends to be a fashion to hysterical symptoms depending on the patient's sex and the times. Presently, women tend to suffer more from severe headaches, weakness or numbness in a particular limb or on one half of the body while back pain is more commonly seen in men and gastrointestinal complaints are more common in children and adolescents. Symptoms also seem to follow a pattern that can best be described as following the patient's body image of his view of how the body functions should be organized rather than the actual physiological organization of the body (Brain, 1969). The doctor must have a clear understanding of neuroanatomy and neurophysiology while examining the hysterical patient. For example, the hysterical patient may describe a constellation of symptoms including weakness on one half of the body associated with numbness and loss of vision, taste, smell, hearing and all other sensory modalities on the same side of the body which would be difficult or impossible to explain on a neurophysiologic basis (Haymaker, 1969). Symptoms such as weakness often involve limbs and other muscular groups predominently under voluntary control and tend to spare the more midline muscular groups such as facial muscles which have many involuntary actions. Hysterical symptoms are always seen as a means to achieve a specific purpose and if delved into during the history, the doctor may obtain some insight into the unconscious motivation of the patient and the psychological mechanisms involved (Brain, 1969). The hysterical patient tends to be very suggestible and if the doctor suggests that he expects a certain symptom to be present along with the other symptoms described by the patient during the history, the patient may accommodate the doctor and indicate that he or she has experienced the suggested symptom. One more symptom is seen as no threat to a patient, but it may be harder to talk a patient out of a particular symptom. Finally, although the hysterical patient suspends critical evaluation and appreciation of his symptoms, he has not suspended the basic survival functions, and hysterical patients will generally not allow the disability to inflict physical harm to themselves. For example, a patient may have hysterical seizures, but will not sustain any injuries and may even show purposeful movements during the seizure in order to prevent injuries such as falling out of bed. Interestingly, the hysterical symptom often has its organic origin in some previous life experience of the patient. During the history, the doctor may discover that the patient once injured the now paralyzed side or possibly a family member was paralyzed or had seizures or had a stroke which in a superficial way resembles the patient's hysterical symptoms. These previous organic disorders may be used as models for the hysterical symptom. The hysterical patient is often perceived by the doctor as being a model patient, that is, a patient who is very cooperative and willing to undergo almost any test or operation with a somewhat naive faith in the doctor. She is often pleasant, even seductive, and may not show any animosity towards her previous doctors or the world in general (DeJong, 1958).

Compared to the hysterical patient, the malingerer is more likely to be a male. Often he has symptoms which he relates to an injury that is potentially compensable and he appears to be angry at what has happened to him. He is quite aware of the extent of his injury and the conscious motivations of his behavior. He may be defensive, hostile or suspicious of examination. His complaints far exceed that expected from the relatively minor injury. This patient does not seem to be motivated towards finding a solution to his problem. The malingering patient is not suggestible as noted with hysterical patients. His symptoms may follow anatomical relationships because they are based ona real injury; however, in an effort to maximize his disability, the patient will often exaggerate and make mistakes in his symptomatology that can easily be discovered by an astute physician. This patient may have had several previous operations or medical treatments, but he appears to be angry about his lack of response to therapeutic modalities. He is often sullen and ill at ease (DeJong, 1958).

Patients with functional overlay tend to be more diverse than either the hysterical or malingering patients, but share some of the characteristics of both. These patients can be male or female, young or old. Like the malingerer, they often come to you angry about their disability and disappointed in previous medical treatment. Similar to the malingerer, there is often an initial injury or illness in the history for which the patient has undergone many forms of medical and/or operative treatment without satisfactory results. Like the hysteric, the motivation behind the disability may be partially or totally unconscious to the patients and they often deny any personal problems. However the doctor may be able to determine that there is a method to their madness during the history and that secondary gains are involved. These patients often see too many doctors and have had too many operations, are on too many medications and have not responded to any of these therapeutic regimes. They will tell you how incompetent their previous doctors were and lead you to believe you are different. You are the specialist and they have come to you for the final solution to their problems. You will soon realize that these patients have a subconscious motivation to maintain their symptoms and unless this motivation is dealt with, you too will be among the unsuccessful in treating their disability. The functional patient is often angry and frustrated. If some form of personality readjustment is not part of the therapy, these patients may improve somewhat under your care, but will either plateau or relapse before they improve to the point of resuming an active and productive life.

Before proceeding to the examination, some general considerations on history-taking should be made that apply to all three groups of psychogenic patients. Interviewing the spouse, parent or other significant person and evaluating their social interaction with the patient is of utmost importance. There may be a lack of concern or over-concern by the significant other person(s) which plays a part in perpetuating the patient's symptoms. Also, the patient's social history becomes quite important to the history—how long has it been since the patient worked, how does he feel about his job and his spouse, how does he see himself and what are his goals in life. Secondly, the astute physician observes the patient from the moment he walks in the door. Introduction and history taking can become part of the physical examination. When a patient is distracted by greetings or during the history, he may use the paralyzed arm to unbutton or take off his coat or give other clues as to the basis of his disorder. In a subtle way, the physician can test hearing, vision, gait, sensation, etc, by simple observation during the history-taking. During the physical examination, we advise the physician to examine the psychogenic patient without the family or friends present. You may be able to trick or confuse the patient or possibly use noxious stimuli to get an adequate response on examination but the family may not understand or appreciate what you are doing. We also advise you to have a chaperone with you when examining a patient of the opposite sex to eliminate any further problems for the physician. Before one can adequately examine the hysterical, malingering or functional patient, the doctor must have a clear understanding of neuroanatomy and neurophysiology. This information is commonly known, especially to a physician in the neurosciences, and is available in many texts. In the bibliography, we will mention a few basic texts concerning neuroanatomy, neuropysiology, neurology, neurologic examination and psychological evaluations (Mayo Clinic, 1976; Brain, 1969; Merritt, 1979; Chusid, 1976; Carpenter, 1978; Gilroy, 1975; Haymaker, 1969). It would be redundant to allude to neuroanatomy and neurophysiology at this time except to mention that a basic knowledge of the following systems is essential—neuroanatomy and neurophysiology of the sensory and motor pathways concerned with peripheral nerves and central nervous system. Also, the physician must have a clear understanding of some of the more common neurologic symptom complexes such as Brown-Sequard Syndrome, syringomyalia, multiple sclerosis, toxic or metabolic neuropathies, thalamic syndrome, frontal lobe disorders, etc, which may in some way vaguely resemble some psychogenic disorders. This understanding will also help the physician know what signs and symptoms to expect to be associated with the presenting signs and symptoms. If these are not found, this raises a question of psychogenic cause for the disorder. Finally, it is important that the physician has some understanding of the psychodynamics and higher cortical and intellectual functioning of the patient in order to evaluate the patient's general intelligence, judgment, mood, affect, memory and interaction with others (Kolb, 1977).

THE NEUROLOGICAL EXAMINATION

The Cranial Nerve Examination

Some of the more common psychogenic symptoms involve this part of the neurologic exam. Signs and symptoms such as dizziness, vertigo, hearing loss, blindness, aphonia or dyspasia, cephalgia, anosmia, etc, are often described by psychogenic patients. Many aspects of cranial nerve dysfunction will be examined in depth in subsequent chapters of this text. Certain neurophysiologic and neuroanatomic relationships, however, must be present to indicate organicity. For example, most psychogenic patients are unaware of the physiology of vision and may show characteristic hysterical response on visual field testing (Weintraub, 1973). They may claim anosmia to a variety of substances which stimulate not only the first, but also may stimulate the fifth and seventh cranial nerves. They may claim total loss of hearing and yet awaken promptly to alarm clocks placed at their bedsides by a somewhat devious physician. Unlike most totally deaf patients, the hysterical patient will talk in a normal tone of voice and may show some response to a sudden unexpected statement from the doctor. Bizarre speech patterns may be noted which are not seen in organic disease. Headaches, dizziness, blurred vision and stiff neck are commonly associated symptoms in both organic and psychogenic patients with normal neurological examination, normal blood pressure, no history of head injury or possibly a history of mild head injury. In these cases, the physician may need to do some testing to rule out the possibility of subarachnoid hemorrhage, meningitis, brain tumor or other organic causes even with a strong suspicion by the physician that he is dealing with a psychogenic patient.

The Sensory Examination

The sensory examination is carried out to discover whether there is an area of absent, decreased, exaggerated or perverted sensation. A sharp pin (Whardenberg wheel) and a tuning fork (128 CPS) are essential instruments. In performing the examination, it is important to remember that vibration and position sensibility are carried to the brain by different pathways than the sensation of pain and temperature and therefore, these modalities must be tested separately. If the patient notes no subjective changes in sensation, the entire body can be tested rapidly. Responses on both sides of the body must be compared. If there are specific sensory symptoms, the examination must concentrate on these areas to delineate the exact area involved. It is important to differentiate between changes due to lesions of the peripheral nerves or nerve roots and those of the central nervous system. In peripheral nerve lesions, the sensory changes should correspond to the distribution of a specific nerve whereas in nerve root lesions, sensory loss has a dermatomal pattern. Lesions of the brainstem or spinal cord cause segmental loss of sensation or a loss below the given level. Lesions in the cerebrospinal axis often cause a disassociation of sensation with loss of certain modalities and preservation of others (Mayo Clinic, 1976; Haymaket, 1969).

There are certain general principles noted in the sensory examination of the psychogenic patient (Brain, 1969; Weintraub, 1977, DeJong, 1958):

1. The sensory loss does not follow neuroanatomical relationships, but rather follows the schema of the patient's image of the organization of the body.

A. A hemisensory loss sharply demarcates at the midline rather than showing zones of sensory sparing which is normally present near the midline.

B. Often there is a sharp demarcation of sensory loss in the limb rather than a more gradual loss of sensation more commonly seen in organic disease. Peripheral sensory losses in a stocking-glove type distribution would be unusual except in ischemic or toxic metabolic polyneuropathies; however, in these organic disorders, the sensory loss will usually be in a more gradual or graded pattern with disassociation between the level of loss of pain and temperature and that of light touch and vibratory sense.

C. Usually all sensory modalities are claimed to be lost in the affected limb, yet the patient may show adequate joint proprioception of the limb on cerebellar testing with finger-to-nose or heel-to-shin testing.

D. The sensory loss in the psychogenic patient is usually more extensive than that seen in organic disease. It may involve the entire limb or one half of the body with loss of pain, temperature, light touch and also possible loss of hearing and vision on the same half of the body. That would be anatomically impossible.

E. The demarcation of the sensory loss in the psychogenic patient usually occurs at the joint space rather than following the sensory patterns seen in radiculopathies and peripheral neuropathies. The sensory loss in the psychogenic patient may be patchy in nature with large skipped areas in the same dermatome. One should keep in mind such entities such as syringomyalia and multiple sclerosis which can be present with unusual patterns of sensory loss. However, in these organic diseases, the loss is more characteristic of an anatomical dermatomal pattern and there are usually other associated signs and symptoms of neurological loss such as motor dysfunction, cerebellar signs and visual loss, etc. leading to the correct diagnosis.

F. Often the psychogenic patients have a sensory loss and motor loss on the same side of the body or involving the same limb. Many peripheral nerves have mixed motor and sensory fibers; however, the associated motor and sensory loss of the psychogenic patient is more extensive than those associated with particular peripheral nerve. The classic spinal cord lesion of the Brown-Sequard syndrome would cause motor loss and loss of touch and vibratory sense on one side and loss of pain and temperature on the other side of the body. Lesions of cortical or subcortical areas may cause sensory and motor loss on the same side of the body; however, there are usually other associated signs and symptoms of organic central nervous system disease and there may be a central facial palsy with preservation of the frontalis muscle on both sides an anatomical relationship that is usually not appreciated by the psychogenic patient.

G. The psychogenic patient may show a sensory loss only on the front half of the body with sparing over the back. This would be impossible.

2. The psychogenic patients are often rather suggestible and can be easily confused.

A. With repeated subtle suggestions, the examiner may be able to influence the signs and symptoms in the psychogenic patient.

B. On repeated examination, there may be a great variation in the sensory loss noted.

C. With repeated fast examination or by crossing the limbs while testing, the psychogenic patient may become confused and induced to vary the sensory exam from side to side. Also, the examiner can examine first the front half of the body and rapidly turn the patient around and examine the back. The patient confuses the sides of the body and shows varying sensory loss.

3. The psychogenic patient, especially the hysteric, may respond to rather naive testing such as the yes-no test; that is, the examiner may ask the patient to close his eyes and respond by no when he does not feel a sensory stimuli. Occasionally, the examiner can obtain no response in the hysterical patient. In order to respond at all, the patient would have to have felt something.

4. The psychogenic patient may not respond to weak stimuli, but as it gradually gets more intense, he may suddenly respond. This is not typical of any disease. Also, the psychogenic patient may respond vigorously to a sudden unexpected noxious stimuli, whereas he may not respond if the same stimuli is given in gradually increasing intensity or if his attention is directed to the stimuli while he is being tested.

5. The psychogenic patient can be tested under hypnosis or hypnotic drugs and in such cases, may show a perfectly normal response to sensory stimuli. While sleeping, the psychogenic patient may move a "paralyzed arm," or show a normal withdrawal response to stimulation with a pin.

6. Usually there is an absence of expected skin changes associated with sensory loss such as sweating, trophic changes, bruises or burns in a patient with a psychogenic sensory loss.

7. Physiologic reflexes are preserved in the psychogenic patient. For example, in Mannhoph's sign, the heart rate will be noted to increase more than ten points with a strong noxious stimuli to an "anesthetic area."

8. The sensory reflexes remain intact in the psychogenic patient. Abdominal, bulbocavernosis and deep tendon reflexes all have a sensory component of the reflex arc and generally are not under voluntary control so they remain intact in the psychogenic patient.

9. The psychogenic patient may not appreciate the

subtle physiologic aspect of the neurologic exam. For example, when a tunning fork is placed over the skull, sternum or other midline bony structure, the patient will deny feeling or hearing the vibration on the anesthetic side of the body when in reality, the vibration is easily transmitted to both sides of the head or body by bone conduction.

10. The psychogenic patient may show unusual responses to sensory stimuli such as hyperesthesia even to the lightest touch and may describe the sensation in vivid terms.

These are some of the characteristics of the psychogenic sensory examination and the astute physician should have no difficulty making the diagnosis if some of the above characteristics are observed. Again, we stress that the physician should continually ask himself if his patient's symptoms could possibly fit any organic disorder such as syringomyelia, multiple sclerosis or toxic metabolic polyneuropathies which may be present with somewhat bizarre findings.

Gait and Station

Normal gait is dependent on intact sensation as well as intact voluntary and associated motor function. The patient should be examined in a standing position with his feet together, first with eyes open and then with eyes closed. He should be observed walking forward, backwards and in tandem gait. In hysterical astasia-abasia, the patient is unable to either stand or walk. However, he has normal muscle tone and motor function when tested in bed. The psychogenic patient may sway from the hips rather than from the ankles when tested in the Romberg position. He may sway as much with his eyes open as with them closed and will show gyrations and a great deal of other associated movements but will not fall or if he does fall, he will not fall to one side consistently and he will not hurt himself. The psychogenic patient with a "hemiplegic gait" will often drag the weak leg behind him in a very theatrical fashion, whereas, brain-injured patients with hemiplegia will have a characteristic circumduction gait with associated spasticity and hyperreflexia. In testing the psychogenic patient with

with gait or station disturbances, he will often have normal cerebellar function, position and vibratory senses, reflexes and will usually show no evidence of brushing or trauma from falls.

The Motor Examination

This part of the examination determines not only the muscle power, but also includes evaluation of muscle tone, bulk, coordination and observation of abnormal movements. Diseases involving the myoneural junction, peripheral nerve roots or anterior horn cells are catagorized as lower motor neuron lesions. Typically these lesions cause weakness that is associated with flaccidity, atrophy of muscle and loss of reflexes. Disease involving motor pathways within the brain or spinal cord cause upper motor neuron paralysis which characteristically has increased muscle tone, spasticity and hyperreflexia. In the motor examination of the psychogenic patient, there are certain general characteristics which can be utilized by the physician to fashion an examination which will help differentiate a psychogenic disorder from a disease with an organic basis:

1. The type of psychogenic symptom may indicate the motivation of the patient. "Occupational neurosis" is a term coined by Lord Brain to describe the motor loss related to a specific activity inherent to the patient's work but not hindering other activities of daily living (Brain, 1969). This type of specific activity motor loss may give the examiner an indication as to the motivation behind the psychogenic symptoms. There is the classic example of the patient who developed an hysterical paraplegia so that she need not attend to an invalid relative. The purpose of the symptom was to prevent her from performing a distasteful duty and yet retain her own self-esteem. No one would expect her to fulfill her duty to an ailing relative if she too were paralyzed.

2. The paralysis does not follow anatomical relationships. Like the psychogenic sensory loss, the motor dysfunction tends to be extensive, involving the entire

limb or possibly half of the body, usually demarcating at a joint space or at the midline of the body and usually with an associated sensory loss on the same side. The psychogenic motor loss usually does not involve only muscle groups innervated by specific nerves or roots.

3. The muscle groups involving primarily voluntary rather than involuntary actions are commonly affected in the psychogenic paralysis. Limbs are often involved.

4. Reflexes are often maintained such as deep tendon reflexes, abdominal reflexes, bulbocavernosis reflexes, gag reflex, corneal reflex and protective reflexive movements. Babinski and other pathologic reflexes are notably absent in apparent upper motor neuron paralysis of psychogenic origin.

5. The motor examination will vary with repeated testing and can be varied by suggestions from the physician. The examiner can subtly suggest that he expects certain muscle groups to be involved jointly with a rather bizarre motor loss whether or not the suggested relationships are truly anatomical and the patient will often fulfill his expectation.

6. The agonist-antagonist relationships of muscles are often maintained. When the psychogenic patient tries to move a limb in the direction of function of the paralyzed muscle, the examiner may feel a contraction of the antagonist muscle, or in the patient with a psychogenic wrist drop, you may ask him to make a fist and the wrist will automatically extend. Such relationships are unknown to the psychogenic patient.

7. Similarly, associated motor actions normally present between muscle groups may be absent in the psychogenic patient. In testing the patient with a "paralyzed lower limb," a Hoover's sign may be elicited; that is, the examiner places his hand under the heel of the normal leg and restrains the patient's attempt to lift the paralyzed leg. Normally in organic paralysis, the patient attempts to life the paralyzed leg by forcing downward with the heel of the opposite normal leg which can be felt by the examiner. In hysterical patients, this is noticeably absent. Likewise, with adduction of the legs if there is no contraction of the adductor in the normal leg with attempted movement of the "paralyzed leg," one must suspect a psychogenic paralysis of the lower limb. Similar testing can be performed on the upper extremities.

8. The hysterical patient, and to some extent the malingering and functional patients, will maintain a protective reflex. If the paralyzed hand is held over the patient's face and dropped, it will automatically swerve to avoid hitting the face. Similarly, the patient with a psychogenic paralysis may take a step or two and then gracefully collapse onto the floor in an attempt to walk but will sustain no injury. As mentioned earlier, no bruising or other evidence of trauma will be noted in such patients and they will show a normal reflexive motor withdrawal to intense, sudden and unexpected stimulation to the paralyzed limb.

9. "You are what you are when you are not watched." It is particularly important in the evaluation of the psychogenic patient to ask nurses, office staff, other medical personnel or even the housekeeping staff to watch a particular patient and ask if the patient moves a "paralyzed limb." When the doctor or family are not present, the patient may be off guard or distracted and may forego his symptoms. It is important to observe the psychogenic patient while asleep or under hypnosis or sedation to observe if he moves the paralyzed limb.

10. In testing motor paralysis in the psychogenic patient, the examiner will often note a characteristic movement of the extremity which gives one the impression the patient is withholding strength. The patient may show varying amounts of effort depending on the force of testing. Also, the patient will initially show effort and then give away with continued testing of the same force. There may be an irregular jerky quality to the patient's voluntary movements not seen in organic disease which typically shows a more smooth and consistent weakness. A psychogenic patient may show no expression at all on testing a weak limb or may show very bizarre and extensive facial grimacing and other associated movements in an attempt to voluntarily move the weak limb. If a paralyzed arm is tested

first with a moderate effort and is then suddenly jerked strongly, reflexive contractions of the "paralyzed" muscle can be felt by the examiner.

11. No atrophy is noted with psychogenic motor loss and there is normal muscle tone in the "paralyzed" muscle unless the symptoms are of long duration and the patient shows some disuse atrophy. Also, generally no fasciculations or other signs of dernervation will be noted in muscles involved in a supposed upper motor neuron paralysis.

12. In less obvious cases, adjunctive testing may be required such as EMG and nerve conduction tests which will be helpful in determining if there is really any organic basis to the weakness.

While examining the psychogenic patient, the physician must constantly ask the question what organic disease could possibly cause this pattern of motor loss. Two key factors which will help the examiner understand the symptoms as being psychogenic rather than organic are: 1. Organic symptoms of motor loss often have other associated neurologic signs and symptoms such as sensory loss, cerebellar findings, and reflex changes. 2. Organic disease may be localized both horizontally and vertically along the neuroaxis. If the examiner does not find the above two factors present, he should begin to consider psychogenic origins for the neurological loss. Multiple sclerosis is always a consideration when one sees a bizarre presentation of symptoms; however, these patients often have a mixture of symptoms involving sensory, motor, cerebellar signs, visual symptoms, etc., and often have a characteristic course of remissions and exacerbations. They may show mental changes but, again, these tend to be rather characteristic. Often they have reflex changes and pathological reflexes, all of which help to separate them from psychogenic groups of patients. Guillian-Barre-Landry syndrome may present with an unusual ascending paralysis or paresis involving either systemic or bulbar musculature; however, these patients often have a rather characteristic pattern to the weakness and progression of their disease and often there are associated signs such as facial diplegia which suggests the diagnosis. Other organic diseases which may in part mimic psychogenic motor loss are ischemic polyneuropathies, diseases of the myoneural junction such as myasthenia gravis, spinal diseases such as syringomyalia or post traumatic spinal cord cysts which may present with motor loss, neoplasms of the brainstem or spinal cord, cerebellar degeneration with associated hypotonia, and many other organic diseases all of which have characteristic presenting signs and symptoms which should prevent the careful examiner from making the important mistake of calling an organic symptom psychogenic and performing a great disservice to the patient (Merritt, 1979; Gilroy, 1975).

DISORDERS OF CONSCIOUSNESS

States of disordered consciousness may occur in either hysteria or malingering. Hysterical loss of consciousness is usually precipitated by emotional distress and is usually very dramatic in onset. These patients appear as though they are in a rather dense coma with no response to verbal or tactile stimulation. This is a withdrawal response to psychological conflict in which the patient presents with a psychogenic image of total body death (Ludwig, 1972). Psychogenic coma is usually diagnosed by the preservation of reflexive neurologic function, normal vital signs, lack of skin changes and normal musculature. The blood pressure will be normal and will increase by at least ten points with noxious stimuli indicating a normal reflexive tachycardia with the stimulation. The eyes will always be closed. The psychogenic body image of death is one with the eyes closed. When the examiner attempts to open the eyes, he will often note a lid spasm or contraction to keep the eyes closed. Doll's eyes and roving eye movements frequently seen in patients in a light coma are commonly absent because of normal cortical inhibition. When the patient's eyes are opened, he may look purposefully towards the examiner, especially if the examiner presents a threatening object within the visual field of the patient. The corneal reflexes will be intact. The cold caloric stimulation testing will also be intact and, being a rather unpleasant stimuli, may arouse the patient from his slumber. Normal nystagmoid eye movements noted with cold calorics will be noted in the psychogenic patient because of adequate cortical functioning. Pupils will be equal and briskly reactive to light. The gag reflex, abdominal reflex, deep tendon reflexes and other normal reflexes will be intact and there will be an absence of pathological reflexes such as the Babinski. A normal withdrawal motor response may be obtained with a sudden sharp, unexpected, noxious stimuli to the feet or hands. Also, with a sudden noxious stimuli such as a nipple pinch, which is totally unexpected by the patient, the examiner may see a purposeful movement of the arm towards the examiner's hand and/or the patient may awaken and clearly state a few well-articulated unpleasantries to the physician. No evidence of trauma is usually noted on these patients. There will be an absence of the characteristic skin changes noted in shock, heat stroke, diabetic coma, etc. Finally, the initial laboratory work such as blood cell count, blood sugar, electrolytes and preliminary toxicology screening will probably all be within normal limits.

Although psychogenic convulsions may resemble organic seizures, they are usually more bizarre in nature and are usually appropriately staged and occur before an audience. The movements are coordinated and purposeful. These patients may clutch at objects or parts of their body and tear off their clothes. The onset of psychogenic fits are more gradual than are seen in a true organic seizure. Often there is no loss of consciousness and when the patient is questioned after the fit, he may remember events that occurred during the fit. Commonly, there is no micturation, no injury to the tongue or other parts of the body with these seizures. The aura, if present, may occur during the seizures rather than preceeding it as they do in organic seizures. Opisthotonus is often seen in psychogenic seizures during the tonic phase. Purposeful movements may be superimposed upon the fit movements in order to prevent injury such as falling out of bed. Usually there is no post-ictal lethargy, paralysis or pathologic reflexes. A sudden unexpected stimuli such as an ice water douche may immediately terminate the fit (Brain, 1969).

CONCLUSION

In this chapter, we have examined some of the historical and physical findings commonly noted in psychogenic disorders. Only portions of the complete neurologic examination have been alluded to as they relate to some of the more common psychogenic symptoms. Using some of these general principles and characteristics described above, we leave it to the astute clinician to fashion his own neurologic examination to fit his particular needs for a particular patient. Repeatedly we have stressed the importance of a clear understanding by the physician of the basic neuroanatomy and neurophysiology in order to manipulate the examination to answer specific questions. Also, the physician needs to obtain a thorough history and perform a complete examination on the patient to avoid being misled by some bizarre signs and symptoms and thereby missing a treatable organic disease. In some cases of somatic disorders, no objective physical signs can be elicited on routine examination and further laboratory testing or specialized examinations may be required. Also, in certain cases with some questionable signs and symptoms or when litigation is involved, further objective tests such as EMG and nerve conduction studies, C.T. Scan, angiograms, lumbar punctures, and psychological testing, may need to be performed. However, it is our hope that some of the information in this chapter may prove to be of value to the physician in making the proper diagnosis and avoid costly tests, surgeries or treatments for psychogenic patients which would only add to their risk and delay proper treatment for their disorder. As a final comment, one of the problems encountered with functional patients is that these patients often have an initial organic problem which has left them with signs and symptoms of organic disease. To this, there may have been added repeated surgeries and other treatments which have left their mark of organic dysfunction. The challenge to the examiner is to sort out that which was organic from that which is functional and to evaluate what proportion each plays in the patient's symptom complex. If a particular patient is like most patients and is suffering mainly from an organic problem but has some underlying anxiety about his disease, he probably will do quite well with surgery or other treatment modalities and return to a happy productive life. If the patient is felt to have equal contributions from the organic and functional components of this disorder, he may do well or at least show significant improvement with surgery or medical treatment and professional psychological assistance. If the patient is mostly functional with only a minor organic component to his problem, he will probably not do well with surgery or other treatment modalities and should be referred for professional psychiatric care or to a multi-faceted clinic such as a pain clinic which specializes in the treatment of such disorders. The art of medicine is in determining where along this spectrum the patient lies. The proper diagnosis and management of these difficult patients is a challenge to the best in our field.

REFERENCES

Brain, Lord and Walton, J.M. *Brain's Diseases of the Nervous System,* Seventh edition. Oxford University Press, London (1969).

Carpenter, M.C. *Core Text of Neuroanatomy,* Second edition. Williams & Wilkins, Baltimore (1928).

Chodoff, P. The Diagnosis of Hysteria, An Overview. *American Journal of Psychiatry,* 131, October 10 (1974).

Chusid, J.G. *Correlative Neuroanatomy and Functional Neurology,* Sixteenth edition. Lange, Los Altos, California (1976).

De Jong, R.M. *The Neurologic Examination,* Second edition. Hoeber-Harper, New York (1958).

Gilroy, J. and Meyer, J.S. *Medical Neurology,* Second edition McMillan Publishing Co., Inc., New York (1975).

Haymaker, W. *Bing's Local Diagnosis in Neurological Disease,* 15th edition. C.V. Mosby Co., St. Louis (1969).

Janet, P. *The Major Symptoms of Hysteria,* Second edition. Macmillan Publishing Co., Inc., New York (1924).

Kolb, L.C. *Modern Clinical Psychiatry.* W.B. Saunders Co., Philadelphia, (1977).
Ludwig, A.M. Hysteria. *Archives of General Psychiatry,* 27, December, (1972).
Mayo Clinic, Rochester, Minnesota. *Clinical Examination in Neurology,* Fourth edition. W.B. Saunders Co., Philadelphia (1976).
Merritt, H.H. *A Textbook of Neurology,* Sixth edition. Lea & Febiger Co., Philadelphia (1976).
Miller, H. Mental Sequelae of Head Injuries. *Proceedings of the Royal Society of Medicine,* 59, 257 (1966).
Plum, F. and Posner, J.B. *Diagnosis of Stupor and Coma,* Contemporary Neurology Series. F.A. Davis Co., Philadelphia (1972).
Weintraub, M. Hysteria. *American Family Physician,* 8, November, (1973).
Weintraub, M. *Hysteria, A Clinical Guide to Diagnosis,* Ciba Clinical Symposia, Volume 19, No. 6, Ciba-Giegy Co., New Jersey (1977).

2
Clinical Examination
For Functional Eye Disease

BRIEN P. JAMES

In ophthalmology, it is often possible to be quite definitive about functional signs. In fact, it is not unusual to find many different ways to substantiate the diagnosis. Put another way, one should strive not to make the diagnosis on a single finding but try to predict and prove collaborating evidence. Patients are seldom totally this or that and therefore, we must attempt to define whether they are, say, 5 percent organic and 95 percent functional or vice versa. By taking a positive attitude, doing an extensive examination, and presenting the findings in a frank way, one can do a great deal of good in shortening the patient's disability and decreasing the cost and risk of the medical workup. Certainly there are the "hard core" patients but the majority of them will be relieved that the cause of their difficulties is not of a more serious nature. Functional disorders of the visual system are most often discussed in a flippant or negative manner. I would like to impart a more practical approach to the problem. Dr. J. Lawton Smith prefers the word "worry" rather than the usual psychological labels. This term is less threatening and encourages the patient towards self-help.

The "functional" response to organic disease should be kept in mind. The physician who tries to do visual fields on a patient with a frontal lobe tumor or contusion probably deserves the verbal abuse he will receive. Fixation difficulties or nondominant parietal lobe involvement are revealed by naming the inability "S.O.B. Syndrome" because the patient not only will not but cannot fixate on a target properly. Paliopsia (preservation of images), teleopsia (illusion that close objects are far away) and hallucinations, formed and unformed, may not be an indication for phenothiazines but rather indications of organic disease.

HISTORY

Quite often, a careful chronological history will make the diagnosis. Statements such as "my mother went blind from glaucoma" or "my uncle died from a brain tumor" reveal concerns which are not unique to the psychogenic patient. Eye complaints in the psychogenic patient may be roughly categorized, but obviously there is a great deal of overlapping of these catagories. The neuro-esthenic patient will complain of multiple mild afflictions such as "eye strain" (whatever that is), fatigue, dryness, watering, blurred vision, photophobia, floaters, after images, spots and sore eyes whereas the complaints of the hysteric will be of a more serious nature but are singular complaints such as amblyopia, diplopia and gaze palsies. It is well know that the most common cause of sudden bilateral blindness is hysteria; however, in my experience, this is seldom seen for it is more often a gradual process. As a general rule, the older the patient, the less likely it is that the symptoms are hysterical. Functional complaints are more common in women. Dr. Thomas Walsh makes the point that monocular difficulties such as amblyopia are more likely related to work and litigation while bilateral involvement is more often seen with hysteria. In compensation cases for example, the employer's reaction to the injury, the time or place of the injury or visual impairment and any previous injuries are quite often revealing. A casual differential diagnosis taken out of context or an overly concerned physician will surely precipitate "worry" in a susceptible patient. An obese young lady with headaches and a "funny looking disc" will lose vision with each eye examination and neuroradiological encounter.

VISION TESTING

Vision testing is done with great care and often with much cheerleading. A refraction is done to rule out myopia, hyperopia, astigmatism and presbyopia. Further examination should rule out motility disorders, nystagmus, cataracts, vitreous and retinal disease, and visual field defects.

Distance vision should be comparable to near vision if organic disease and refractive errors are ruled out. The eight-year-old school girl who desires glasses to complement her orthodontures will, when asked if she can read the chart, respond "yes, but—not—ver-ry—well." She is best refracted in the trial frame, slowly decreasing the induced "fog" stepwise with small lenses and with each change, encouraging her to read just one more letter or just one more line. Usually by the time the lenses are neutralized or if there is nothing in the trial frame, she is reading 20/20. The trial frame is then removed and one politely reveals the fallacy of her presumed blurred vision.

Testing near vision is done in a similar way. Starting with the print so large that even the most obstinate patient will have to admit seeing it, the magnification is slowly increased stepwise while encouraging the patient each time to read the next smaller line, word or letter. What the patient does not know is that four diopters of convex lenses will magnify two times. By adding small powered lenses successively, they cannot deny that there is magnification and that it is easier to read, but they do not know mathematically how much better it should be. They will succumb to reading the finest print before they should. If the above methods do not suffice, one must resort to more drastic measures. Optokinetic responses are an involuntary reflex. Some knowledgable people can stare through the targets so they should be performed horizontally and vertically. Large targets demonstrate about 20/200 vision. The common cloth measuring tapes represent probably about 20/70 vision. There is an obvious discrepancy if a patient cannot read 20/400 but an optokinetic response is elicited with a small tape.

If a mirror is held in front of a patient who professes blindness, and he is instructed not to move his eyes, any twist of the mirror will elicit eye movement if vision is present. If a ruler is interposed halfway between the eyes and reading material and the edge is perpendicular to the reading matter, the ability to read should be interrupted if there is monocular "blindness." It is said that some examiners have even resorted to printing obscenities on flash cards to elicit a response from a "blind" patient.

The various ways to check monocular blindness are legend. Included are the use of red and green lenses with red and green print, polarized lenses with polarized print, pinholes and prisms. Refixation of an eye after a prism is removed implies good vision. Under cycloplegia, a near correction (+ 2.50) is placed over the affected eye leaving a distance correction over the good eye. Then quickly, before the patient can close one or the other eye in order to discover the ruse, ask him to read far and then near.

PUPILLARY EXAMINATION

The most important sign in the visual examination is the Marcus Gunn pupil, variously called pseudo-Marcus Gunn pupil, afferent pupil, swinging light test and curtsy pupil by the British. A Marcus Gunn pupil occurs if the direct pupillary response to light is less than the consensual light response from the other eye. It is best performed in subdued room light with a bright examining light. A common error is to confuse pupillary slip for a Marcus Gunn pupil. The very first or immediate pupillary reaction to the direct light determines whether it is a Marcus Gunn pupil. Slight or "1 +" reactions are difficult to call. The point is that if a patient states he cannot see out of an eye and there is no Marcus Gunn pupil, one must be suspicious of functional disease. A Marcus Gunn pupil is present if there is any, even minimal, optic nerve disease or with severe retinal disease. Minimal optic neuritis, even with 20/20 vision, will display a Marcus Gunn pupil. Conversely, macular disease with 20/200 vision probably will not have the Marcus Gunn pupil. If the pupil is fixed and immobile in an involved eye secondary to disease, one may gain information if the consensual response in the uninvolved eye is less than the direct response; that is, if when doing the "swinging light" test, the uninvolved pupil markedly constricts over the consensual response. By definition, one cannot have bilateral Marcus Gunn pupils because the phenomenon relies on the comparison of relatively normal responses, direct and consensual to abnormal responses.

Functional pupillary disorders when not accompanied by constriction with convergency are those induced by drugs. Sometimes functional or malingering patients will instill Atropine in one eye to cause pupillary dilation. To differentiate an Atropine pupil in the functional patient from a dilated pupil secondary to an organic neurologic disorder, the instillation of Pilocarpine will cause the latter to constrict. Drs. Smith and Daroff encountered a perplexing nurse who instilled Atropine in one eye and Pilocarpine in the other.

MOTILITY

Functional motility problems are rather uncommon. A condition that is seldom believed by the physician and patient alike is "spasm of the near reflex" as described by Cogan and Freese. The patient over-converges, producing a miotic pupil, and it must be differentiated from a host of pseudo-sixth nerve palsies. The accomodative spasm often is fluctuating, with induced myopia, and can be accompanied with micropsia. The hallmark sign is the miosis produced by lateral gaze.

This condition has been described with encephalitis; Lues and I have observed it with the intranuclear ophthalmoplegia in dissemenated sclerosis. It is more often seen with trauma to the head (baseballs) and with flat overcorrected contact lenses. The functional patient will have spasm of the near reflex without the above diagnoses and may even have a functional nystagmus superimposed. Treatment is best with a short course of cycloplegic drops.

Blepharospasm, while most often on an organic basis, may be a sign of functional overlay. Most childhood periorbital tics appear to be of an identification or attention-getting etiology. Decreased ability to see near objects and sometimes diplopia at near vision can be a functional disorder. If no near reflex of the pupil is elicited with a good near object, a functional etiology should be suspected. As usual, organic causes such as Parkinsonism must be eliminated. Once in a while, one will encounter "gaze palsies" after minor trauma at work. A sudden display of twenty dollar bill in the appropriate area can be revealing.

NYSTAGMUS

A nystagmus is sometimes diagnosed as functional when in truth it is one of the rare forms of organic nystagmus. A true functional (voluntary) nystagmus is quite rapid and cannot be maintained for more than a few seconds and is accompanied by convergence of the eyes. In reality, this is a parlor trick but some individuals may try to impress you with the fact that it occurred after a minor mishap. The neurologic follow of an injured worker may be confused by his having congenital nystagmus. A congenital nystagmus is reconized when it is horizontal in up-gaze, has a null point, dampens with convergence, increases with fixation, changes with optokinetic targets, and may have a latent nystagmus component superimposed. The diagnosis of congenital nystagmus in these cases will shorten the hospital stay and decrease the neurodiagnostic workup.

VISUAL FIELDS

Again, history leads one to anticipate certain visual field disorders. Loss of depth perception, especially at night, may suggest a bitemporal defect. A relative may volunteer that the patient always drives down the middle of the road, or to one side of the road or other. They may have difficulty with reading, following the line, or trouble picking up the beginning of the next line, which can suggest a hemianopic defect. While one sees transient constrictions of visual fields with migraine, a fluctuating field suggests a functional disorder, especially when associated with regression of images.

Dr. Hoyt has pointed out that when doing confrontation fields, functional patients will often respond to seeing the hand when the examiner's elbow is at 90 degrees. The examiner then backs off from the patient and repeats the hand movements. The patient will again prefer the 90-degree elbow, confirming a tubular hysterical field. Tangent screens and perimeters are both useful in functional visual field testing, especially by comparing red targets with white. If the examiner can suggest a visual field that is the same size or larger with red targets as was obtained with white targets, he has objective proof of a functional disorder. Though unusual, functional hemianopic defects can be unmasked in this way. Functional visual fields are noted for being susceptible to suggestion. With encouragement and persistence, the fields may enlarge or constrict. A square test object can at times elicit a square visual field. The classical functional field is tubular constriction, that is, the same size of field at one and two meters. Spiralling fields are not as common but are manifestations of a functional disorder.

One should not forget that these fields can also be elicited in debilitated patients and in frontal temporal lobe disease. Scotomas are generally incompatible with the diagnosis of hysteria. Reviewing the previous fields will often show the progressive constriction with each succeeding angiogram, lumbar puncture and visual examination.

The examiner's positive attitude with the complete and documented examination and the full explanation to the patient are the hallmarks of the clinical examination of the functional patient. In this way, one may most often shorten the medical workup and relieve the "worried" patient of his symptoms.

Ashworth, Bryan. *Clinical Neuro-ophthalmology.* Blackwell Scientific Publications, Victoria, Australia (1973).

Lessell, Simmons. Higher disorders of visual function: negative phenomena, in *Neuro-ophthalmology,* Volume III, Flasser, Noel S. and Smith, J. Lawton, eds. The C.V. Mosby Co., St. Louis (1975).

Smith, J. Lawton. *The Optic Nerve*, Miami, Fla. (1977).

Walsh, Thomas. *Neuro-ophthalmology, Clinical Signs and Symptoms*. Lea & Febiger, Philadelphia (1978).

Walsh, Thomas and Hoyt, William F. *Clinical Neuro-ophthalmology*, Third Edition. Williams & Wilkins Co., Baltimore (1969).

3
Hearing, Balance, and Speech
WILL P. PIRKEY

The differential diagnosis between hysteria and organic disease affecting hearing, balance and speech, can be difficult and time-consuming. Although hearing, balance and voice can be interdependent, they will be discussed separately in this chapter. For this discussion, no distinction will be made between willfull malingering and classical hysterical or psychogenic deafness. In other words, the entire range of non-organic hearing loss, imbalance and speech disorders are covered. These conditions can affect any age and may vary with the era. It tends to be worse during wars, time of impending conflicts, and during times of both national and individual stress.

PSYCHOGENIC HEARING LOSS

In all probability psychogenic hearing loss affects approximately 4–5 percent of all people complaining of hearing loss. There is often a functional overlay on a true organic loss which must be kept in mind. In fact, functional overlay is more frequently found with an actual organic loss than in a normal hearing person.

Proper diagnosis is of upmost importance. Seldom it is made from one or two test results, but from the interpretation of a battery of examinations and tests. A careful history and physicial examination often can suggest a psychogenic overlay. Such observations as the following should be noted:

HISTORY

1) Discrepancy between otological findings and history
2) Degree of loss incompatible with history and otological finding
3) Rapidly progressive loss without evidence of organic disease
4) Total deafness with normal vestibular response
5) Unilateral loss without clear etiology
6) Obvious psychiatric disorder
7) Sudden onset of total binaural deafness
8) Normal response to questioning during caloric tests
9) Unsolicited comments or questions regarding compensation
10) Discrepancy between stated history and medical records
11) Remarks such as, "I can get along fine when I can read your lips. My ears ring so much I can't hear the tones. The ringing in my ears confuse me. I don't do well on these tests, I don't see how a test with tones will tell you how much trouble I have. I don't care about the money–it's my hearing that counts. My hearing fluctuates a lot. The doctor thought I was faking."

Manner of Listening—Speaking

1) Exaggerated attempt to hear
2) Exaggerated staring - attempt to impress with ability to lip read
3) Discrepancy between history and articulatory and phonating pattern
4) Excessively loud voice
5) Refusal to attempt lip reading - may force examiner to write
6) Discrepancy between lip reading ability and hearing loss history

Hearing Aid Usage

1) Wears weak aid while professing severe loss
2) Wears aid turned off or with insignificant degree of volume
3) Claims regular use of aid, but aid shows no signs of wear
4) Claims severe loss, but wears no aid

5) Claims regular aid use, but with no clear idea of cost of batteries

6) Claims improper improvement or no improvement from hearing aid or from therapy

Miscellaneous

1) Obvious nervousness - increases as test progresses
2) Failure to keep appointment
3) Alcohol odor or drunkenness

The most diagnostic signs of non-organic hearing loss are a result of discrepancies between two pieces of information. One must first be aware of, and recognize, the proper relationship between various examinations and tests. There is a striking similarity among the responses of the vast majority of patients with organic hearing loss. The responses of the average functional patient stand out in sharp contrast. Most patients with functional deafness, whether from malingering or hysteria, respond in essentially the same manner to pure tone or speech tests.

Perhaps the most frequent clue to functional hearing loss is a fluctuation in threshold on repeated pure tone testing. Serous otitis media and cochlearhydrops may bring about fluctuation in pure tone thresholds similar to those caused by functional deafness. However, history and physical examination can usually differentiate these conditions.

In addition to repeated pure tone hearing tests, other acoustic tests can alert the physician to a probably functional hearing loss. Such tests include:

ACOUSTICAL EXAMINATION

Tuning Fork Tests

1) Incompatible with history or physical exam
2) No lateralization or indefinite responses
3) Becker bone conduction test—failure to transfer Weber test should lateralize to occluded ear
4) Variation in responses to Rinne' & Schwabach on repeated tests

5) Responds only momentarily to tone
6) Denies hearing fork but responds to audiometer between 50 to 60 dB

Pure Tone Audiometric Test

1) Variation in pure tone threshold
2) Variation between pure tone test results and stated history, and between pure tone test results and ability to discriminate either PB test or in general conversation
3) Saucer audiogram
4) Incompatability between bone conduction threshold and discrimination score
5) Immediate increase in stability and responses following mentioning to patient of "unusual variations"
6) Slow, deliberate, obviously thoughtful response
7) Bone conduction equally depressed 20-40 dB for all frequencies
8) Slight movement in fingers or hand prior to giving voluntary response to tone
9) Bone conduction significantly poorer than air conduction
10) Winces in pain to intense sound but refuses to respond voluntarily
11) Improvement in unoperated ear following stapedectomy

Speech Audiometer Test

1) Half-word response to spondee tests; the half-word response may have no relation to its relative phonetic power; often given with rising inflection.
2) Hesitation and obvious deliberation before giving a response to spondee
3) Misses spondee at every lead
4) Fluctuating Speech-Reception Threshold (SRT)
5) Discrepancy between best monaural SRT and free field SRT
6) Responds to questions with ease, but will not repeat spondee at same level
7) Responds without error to both spondee and PB tests at between 90 & 100 dB, with final thresholds of 80-90 dB
8) Symmetrical bilateral puretone loss but significant variation in discrimination score

Special Tests

1) Psycho-galvanic Skin Response (PGSR)
2) Brainstem Auditory Evoked Response (BAER)
3) Doerfler-Stewart Test
4) Delayed Speech Playback Test (DAF)
5) Stenger & Modified (speech) Stenger
6) Swinging voice or story test
7) Lombard Test

Methodology and interpretation of the results from these tests are given in the following section of this chapter.

DEFINING EXTENT OF HEARING LOSS

With the increasing numbers of patients seeking compensation due to automoblie accidents, work injury, noise exposure, drug reactions and the traumas associated with everyday life, it is essential that the degree of organic hearing loss be determined.

Two questions are of paramount importance:

1) What is the degree of organic hearing loss?
2) What is the cause of the hearing loss?

The degree of organic hearing acuity is frequently difficult to determine. Each case is unique, making it impossible to describe specific procedures for determining actual threshold levels. Three groups of procedures, when appropriately combined, will usually give a reasonably valid measure of the degree of organic hearing present. They are:

1) Counseling
2) Repeated testing, both pure tone and speech
3) Special tests adapted for use in functional testing

The majority of individuals who attempt a functional loss, do so with half-determination or half-conviction. Most of these patients will give up the non-organic aspects of their loss if provided the opportunity and offered a little motivation. Approximately two-thirds of all cases found to have a nonorganic hearing loss can be induced to give up that loss through counseling. Approached in an understanding manner, most of these persons will voluntarily provide valid and reliable responses and seem relieved to be able to do so. A functional loss of conscious origin usually cannot be removed, however, without providing the patient with a "graceful way out." This is fundamental in an examination designed to provide a measure of organic hearing acuity. It is helpful to give him a chance to say he did not understand the directions, or that he was very tired and will be able to perform better next time, etc. It must be kept in mind that the task is to obtain valid and reliable thresholds and not to imply to the patient that there has been some conscious fabrication on his part.

In many patients diagnosed as functionally deaf where suggestions and counseling are not effective in substantially improving the thresholds, measures of organic acuity may be approached through simple repetition of speech and pure tone audiometric examinations. Repetition of the tests serves to demonstrate that the examiner is seriously concerned with the manner in which the examination is progressing. In addition, it tends to confuse the patient and disrupts his ability to remember reference levels. Repeated pure tone tests are particularly effective when the audiometer used has a continuously variable frequency. If the hearing loss dial on such an audiometer is set at 5 to 10 dB below the admitted threshold at a given frequency and a "sweep" toward that frequency is begun from a higher frequency, the person with a functional overlay usually will get a sensation of increasing intensity. If the gradually changing frequency is heard and if there is a sensation of increasing loudness, the patient may respond to the tone at an intensity level he previously denied hearing. Each time a new threshold is established, the hearing loss dial should be set down another 5 to 10 dB and the sweep continued. A pure tone procedure of this type, if persistently used for many minutes, may result in such confusion of reference level that the patient voluntarily will begin to respond in an accurate manner.

There are several special tests which may be used in an effort to determine thresholds of organic hearing acuity:

1) Stenger Test
2) Delayed Speech Playback Test
3) Competing Messages Test
4) The Brainstem Evoked Response
5) Doerfler-Stewart Test

The Stenger Test is based on the fact that if two stimuli, varying only in intensity, are presented simultaneously to both ears the patient will be aware of hearing the stimulus only in the ear hearing it the louder. A masking effect takes place which makes the patient unaware of the presence of a lesser stimulus in the opposite ear. This principle has been used with both pure tone and speech stimuli. The pure tone and modified (speech) Stenger Tests have been used successfully in patients with unilateral deafness, especially as a diagnostic tool. If the Stenger Test is further modified to include some element of confusion, it can be used as a threshold-seeking device for testing persons with a bilateral hearing loss. Confusion and anxiety may be developed by requiring the patient to respond to a mixture of live voice two-syllable words (spondees) and appropriate personal questions. At the same time he is repeating spondees and answering questions about himself and his hearing loss he should be requested to indicate by hand signals the ear in which the spondees are heard, i.e., the dominant ear. The patient must be kept under constant pressure to respond and consequently given little opportunity to reflect on his functional reference level. The relative intensity of the speech should be gradually and occasionally rapidly varied so that first one ear is dominant and then the other. The intensity of the speech in both ears should be kept close to the most recently admitted thresholds; slightly above the admitted threshold in one ear and slightly below in the other. While the relative intensity between the ears is being varied, there should be a steady decrease in the overall intensity of the speech in each ear. The channel interrupters (left-right ear selectors) should be used frequently. When the patient has become thoroughly confused and aware that a gradual decrease in the overall intensity of the speech has taken place in both ears, and that he has responded to speech at a level previously denied, he usually will cease responding altogether or gradually give up the functional portions of his hearing loss. In either case, the test will have proved of value. At the least, the examiner will have obtained information which he can use during the counseling sessions. Ideally, however, he will be able to locate the threshold of organic hearing acuity. There are virtually unlimited variations which may be included in this general procedure. In addition to the Stenger, and these modifications of the Speech Stenger, the Delayed Speech Playback Test is an excellent tool for use with functional hearing loss problems. The Delayed Speech Playback Test requires that the patient read out loud some relatively simple material. As he is reading, his speech is recorded and, through earphones, played back to him after a brief delay. When the "delayed speech" is heard by the patient at possible 20 dB above his true organic speech reception threshold, his normal speech patterns are interfered with. In some cases, the patient finds it impossible to continue reading. The Delayed Speech Playback is best adapted for testing persons with relatively flat hearing losses. When there is a functional overlay to a sharply falling high tone organic loss this test may be expected to produce less than satisfactory results due to the variable effect loudness increase has on speech discrimination.

BSER, or Brainstem Evoked Response testing with the averaging computer has advanced to the point that thresholds of hearing may be approximated. This, being an entirely involuntary test, can be very informative and is discussed in further detail in another chapter.

IMBALANCE

Patients complaining of imbalance or dizziness make this complaint when they are uncertain of their position or motion in relation to the environment. Dizziness in its broadest sense is a disorder of human spacial orientation, rather than a particular disease entity. Although vestibular disease is a common cause, more than one half of the cases are caused by other actual causes. A psychogenic, or psychogenic related cause, such as hyperventilation, is a frequent etiologic factor.

Again, the diagnosis of functional or hysterical dizziness is made by the patients' inconsistency and non-physiological responses to questioning and testing.

History

1) Symptoms often present for many years (5–10)
2) Symptoms are continuous, not intermittent or episodic
3) Patient has associated feelings of panic, fright, remoteness, depression, and prespiration
4) Difficulty in concentrating
5) Loss of energy, interest, appetite, and fatigue
6) Patients respond to most or none of series of dizziness
7) Stimulation tests (feeling of floor rising and falling)
8) Failure to fit any psychologic pattern
9) Secondary somatic preoccupation as a result of the long standing, poorly understood, disability produced by their dizziness

Symptoms are not crisp—they do not conform to known pathological characteristics. They may be "drunken walking," "room circles," "staggering," "loss of consciousness for 2–3 minutes."

Both E.N.G. and infrared photoelectric recording have been used to many years and are well understood, and will not be discussed.

Test Battery

1) Blood Pressure—lying and standing (immediate and in 3 minutes)
2) Valsalva Maneuver
3) Carotid sinus stimulation

4) Head turn, sitting and standing, eyes open and closed
5) Sudden turn while walking
6) Hyperventilation—3 minutes
7) Nylen-Barany Test
8) Barany Rotation Test
9) Ask patient to perform other maneuvers that trigger his own dizziness
10) Rhomberg
11) Neurologic Examination

Special Test

1) Electronystagmography, using either air or water, bithermal either individually or simultaneously
2) Infrared Photoelectric
3) Vestibular Nerve Evoked Response
4) Turning
5) Computes Balance
6) CAT Scan
7) Thyroid Panel
8) 5-hour glucose tolerance test
9) Food allergy studies

Vestibular Evoked Response is not a widely used method of determining labyrinthine function. LaVar Best has developed a test using V.E.R. and has had extensive experience with it. Its validity in determining labyrinthine function has been convincingly proven to the clinicians.

Sinusoidal Harmonic Acceleration Test is the most sophisticated and scientific of the vestibular tests. A vestibulargram can be plotted using varying frequencies of stimulation, thus giving the most accurate total vestibular response available at present. This is accomplished without the distraction of discomfort from temperature of air or water, and markedly decreased somatic responses.

The determination of a differential diagnosis of functional balance problems is even more complex than differentiating functional hearing problems. Functional balance problems are often determined by a process of exclusion. If the labyrinth appears to function normally, if no evidence of central nervous system disease is found, and if the history is suggestive, the diagnosis of a functional balance problem is often made. The patient must have follow-up. Small tumors can be very difficult to locate; certain central nervous system disease can be very confusing and can be impossible to correctly diagnose in its early stages. As continuing research on the central nervous system expands our knowledge of the vestibular system, this uncertainty will, hopefully, be lessened.

SPEECH

Functional speech disorders are even less understood. Although the diagnosis and treatment of laryngeal disease, structural anomalies and physiological disorders are not major problems, there is often a major problem in understanding the relationship between voice disorders and associated laryngeal conditions. Vocal sounds are directly related to specific patterns of vocal cord vibration. These patterns may be modified voluntarily or by physiological or psychological disease. But it is the vibration and not the disease itself that determines the sound. This means that laryngeal disease cannot be diagnosed on the basis of the sound or lack of sound produced. Laryngeal disease does not reveal itself in the vocal sound until it alters vocal cord vibration.

The behavioral and psychological deviations from the norm, as they are expressed in communicative disorders, are not well recognized or treated. Major voice anomalies, such as: 1) aphonia, 2) stuttering, and 3) spastic aphonia have been considered functional in origin for many years. There are some findings now questioning the inclusion of spastic aphonia; but the mild and disturbing changes claimed by singers, actors, public speakers and ordinary citizens, when no laryngeal reason can be found, add another dimension to the differential diagnosis. Again, history is very important in the differential diagnosis. Inconsistency between history, physical findings and test results is the most diagnostic factor. An evaluation using these several procedures would be as follows:

History

1) The sudden loss of voice while in conversation
2) The momentary loss of voice or change in voice
3) The loss of voice while talking with strangers, over the telephone, when meeting new people
4) Lack of other symptoms associated with acute infection, chills, fever, painful throat
5) History of the first symptoms occurring in association with or following an emotional or stressful situation
6) The total loss of voice—usually sudden in onset
7) Spontaneous remission
8) Any therapy, providing physician shows interest and caring attitude, may often help, or has helped in past

Physical Examination - Indirect or Direct

1) Examination of larynx shows no vocal cord edema, injection or new growth
2) Examination shows equal vocal cord movement
3) Both abduction and adduction or cords equal, but a bilateral and equal bowing of the cords (a failure of the cords to tense) may be present
4) Patient is often very difficult to examine adequately with a mirror, without complete local anesthesia and patience

Special Tests

1) X-ray of larynx with cinephotography may show equal cord movement. No delay, or evidence of mass in either cord.
2) Stroboscopic examination may show gross movements equal, but may see fine quivering of both cords.
3) E.M.G. shows normal neuromuscular response
4) Photography with high-speed motion picture camera may show normal movement.

Functional or non-organic changes in the voice, if allowed to continue for any length of time, can become very difficult to overcome. It is, therefore, important to carefully examine the vocal cords in motion. Carefully question the patient concerning emotional or stressful situations preceeding onset of symptoms. The help of a voice therapist should be considered. Always remember that the patient must be given a "graceful way out." Counseling is usually necessary. In most areas this is best done by a voice specialist. If none is available, a speech therapist with special interest and training in voice problems and laryngeal behavior should be used.

In all of the questionable hearing, balance or voice disturbances, do not forget the importance of the psychiatrist, or of the clinical psychologist.

REFERENCES

Katz, Jack. *Handbook of Clinical Audiology,* second ed. Williams & Wilkins Co., Baltimore (1978).

Rose, Darrell E. *Audiological Assessment.* Prentice-Hall Inc., Englewood Cliffs (1971).

Neurological Evaluation of the Psychogenic Patient

4
Reliability of
Neuroradiologic Diagnosis

CHARLES E. SEIBERT

Unfortunately, radiological exams cannot be relied upon to differentiate patients with hysterical symptoms from those with organic disease. Patients with hysterical symptoms may have positive x-ray findings and, on the other hand, patients with proven disease may have negative radiological exams. My contribution here is to summarize the types of neuroradiological studies that may be of help in the clinical exam, estimate degrees of accuracy and confidence levels of neuroradiologic diagnosis, outline potential risk of x-ray exposure, and summarize efficacy and cost relationships.

One of the problems facing the examining physician with a patient with a suspect neurological disorder is the myriad of potential tests available. Of these available studies various neuroradiological tests are often ordered and these include the following radiographic exams:

Skull and Cervical Spine; Tomograms of Cervical Spine, or special portions of the skull, e.g., petrous pyramid tomograms; Flexion extension dynamic studies of the spine; Computerized tomography; Nuclear Radiological Procedures, Isotope Brain Flow Scan, and Isotope Static Brain Scan. Contrast studies including angiography, pneumoencuphalography, myelography, discography, and epidural venography.

It is obvious that not all or even a small number of patients presenting with a variety of subjective complaints of potential disease deserves any or a portion of the above-mentioned studies. In fact, many thoughtful medical observers would argue that the pursuit of a cause for subjective complaints in the absence of objective neurological or neurosensory findings is an expensive exercise in "diagnostic overkill." On the other hand, it is well known that an occasional patient will only have a subjective complaint such as headache yet harbor a curable and potentially seious lesion such as a meningioma. Fortunately, this situation is uncommon.

In the allotted space I will attempt to pick several common symptom complex areas and discuss the pertinent radiological exams and limits of accuracy in confidence levels of diagnosis with negative or positive findings on x-ray studies. I have chosen to discuss headache, dizziness, and neck or back pain.

HEADACHE

It is often difficult to separate the symptoms and symptom complex of headache from cervical spine pain, but since headache is probably the most common complaint referable to the body above the neck, I will attempt to describe the radiographic studies in its workup. My first assumption is that a detailed history, physical and neurological exam has been done. A radiological examination such as a skull series is designed as a consultation in response to referral of a patient with a problem and a specific symptom complex, but in another sense we are screening for the presence of disease within the cranial cavity. Many of the x-ray procedures which I will describe are often used as screening procedures; however, many do not meet the necessary criteria for a good screening exam which are: (1) a screening procedure should be painless and safe, (2) should be readily available at low cost, and (3) it must have a high degree of accuracy and a low number of false positives.

The efficacy of a negative test is difficult or impossible to quantify but nevertheless the importance of a negative test should not be underemphasized. We still see a large number of worried well patients who hope only to pass their tests. Normal or negative studies or tests often yield immediate benefits to patients from an increased feeling of well being. The social and economical impact of large-scale testing is significant, and for this reason I cannot advocate liberal screening techniques using radiographic exams at the present time.

The traditional first radiological exam used on the patient with a headache has been a skull x-ray series but I would raise the question now as to be wisdom of continuing this practice. A skull x-ray series has been traditionally used as the mainstay of admission diagnosis because it conveyed the opportunity for inspection of the cranial bony vault for disease and for secondary abnormalities such as thickening of bone, erosion of bone, or hyperostosis. It gave secondary information as to the presence or absence of a mass lesion within the skull which might displace normal calcified structures from the midline such as the pineal and, finally, it might give secondary findings that would suggest chronic increased intracranial pressure secondary to a mass lesion within the skull and with changes on the bone or the sutural linings of the skull because of the secondary changes from increased intracranial pressure. In 1936 Sussman reviewed 333 brain tumor suspects, and of these from a very selected series of workup diagnoses 156 harbored tumors, and of these 47 percent had primary or secondary findings on the plain films of the skull (Kieffer, 1979). This might seem to be a relatively good yield; however, in actuality it represents an extremely low yield of positive diagnoses. This feeling has been borne out by recent reviews. Thus, the plain skull film x-ray series has a relatively low field of information and is only positive in low numbers even in a highly suspect patient population for intracranial disease. What then is a more logical diagnostic technique in the patient suspected of intracranial disorder? The two examinations that quickly come to mind are the radionuclide brain flow and brain scan and the computerized tomographic study of the brain and cranium.

In the radionuclide study a radioactive isotope is injected into the blood stream, circulates about the body and its activity is recorded on a sensing device known as a gamma camera. This instrument is able to detect the actual flow of the isotope to the brain and scalp and skull in a dynamic fashion, thus an assessment of the circulation to the brain is possible. The static brain scan is also then performed which allows study of the integrity of the linings of the brain and structure of the brain or the blood brain barrier. Lesions of the brain such as a stroke or a brain tumor cause disruptions in the blood brain barrier and give an area of increased activity or isotope localization, thus a positive brain scan. The limitation of the isotope brain scan is obvious in that the actual structure of the normal brain structures or subtle abnormal brain structures is not apparent and lesions or abnormalities must disrupt the blood brain barrier or have had abnormal circulatory patterns to provide a positive test; therefore, many isotope examinations will be false negative studies. The risk is very low and the radiation exposure is similarly minimal.

Computerized tomography, a relatively new technique, designed and instituted into clinical practice in 1973, has proven to be quantum leap forward in neuroradiological diagnosis. In this technique an x-ray source and a detector system rotate about the patient's cranium with the x-ray beam in a slit-like fashion projected across a plane of the skull. The varying degrees of x-ray exposure and absorption are detected by the detector system on the opposite side of the brain and cranium and this information of absorption levels in fed into a computer. Because of the rotation of the apparatus about the patient's head multiple angular absorptions are recorded and detected and the computer can mathematically determine what kinds of densities had to be present within the cranium to yield the kind of absorptions that had been transmitted. The computer then maps, records and projects a visual, diagramatic, pictorical representation of the intracranial contents, so that the brain is depicted in slices like the leaves in a book; but the anatomy is faithfully reproduced and normal anatomy as well as pathological disease states are accurately delineated. The examination may be repeated following the injection of an iodine containing contrast material which circulates within the blood system and because of the molecular weight of the iodine, this heavier material is detected by the computer system and the x-ray absorption and is identified within vascular structures which may be normal or abnormal; thus, tumors or areas of stroke or abnormal vascularity may be accurately delineated.

What, then, is the relative contribution of radionuclide studies and/or computerized tomography of the brain? Perhaps the most meaningful method of reviewing the contribution is to review the numbers of examinations that have been requested by physicians, since volume studies are in a sense a methodology for review of the physician's attitude towards contribution to diagnosis of these exams. A recent review of statistics at Massachusetts General Hospital showed a decrease such that since the advent of computerized tomography there was a decrease in radionuclide isotope brain scan studies of 41 percent, a decrease in angiography of 50 percent, and a 73 percent decrease in the numbers of pneumoencephalography. It appears, therefore, that physicians are using computerized tomography in place of nuclide studies, encephalographic studies, and angiographic studies (Fineberg et al, 1977).

Computerized tomography allows a much more efficient use of the health dollar which may prevent a need for hospital expansion because a significant number of patients will no longer have to be admitted for investigations as note above with the decreased number of PEG and angiography. Estimates as to the accuracy of nuclear medicine studies and/or computerized tomography vary, but it is generally accepted that the overall accuracy of the nuclide scan is in the range of 80. 90 percent and that computerized tomography studies' accuracy are in the range of 90. 95 percent. If both examinations are done the accuracy can approach 100 percent. I certainly would not advocate the use of both of these studies in each patient but there are occasions in which the nuclide study can be helpful following a negative or confusing computerized tomogram. The majority of these situations involve differential diagnosis of stroke and in the occasional patient with an unusual meningioma. Some examiners would state the case more emphatically (Duboulay and Marshall, 1975). Duboulay reviewed 897 patients who had nuclide studies done, of which 290 also had CT examinations done, and concluded that no case nor justification could be made of the nuclide study in whom a patient would have a computerized tomography (Duboulay and Marshall, 1975).

Nadich offers a probably more practical approach to the use of computerized tomography in the brain and suggests the following (Nadich et al., 1978): Patients with typical tension headaches or uncomplicated migraine do not need any radiographic examinations. Patients with headaches of uncertain origin should have computerized tomography to exclude an organic lesion, and patients with severe migraine or migraine with neurological sequelae should have computerized tomography to exclude aneurysm, AV malformation, and to evaluate the extent of migraine atrophy, edema, or infarction. Patients with headache and a subsequently normal CT are observed without further workup. A radionuclide scan can be of use in the diagnosis of an AV malformation or in small convexity meningioma, and may also be of value when iodine allergy exists preventing the use of contrast material in computerized tomography. Nadich concludes that CT should replace the radionuclide scan and the skull series as initial diagnostic exams in patients with neurological abnormalities. Finally, the exception to the use of direct referral for CT instead of skull radiographic exams is in patients in whom pituitary lesions or other lesions in and about the sella arc suspect. In these patients—and those represent a small number—skull radiographs as the initial films are still recommended, since at present limitations of detail in the base of the brain with computerized tomography limits its comtribution in this area. This latter observation is currently in a state of change and in all probability will change in the next two years with the advent of improved, more detailed computerized tomographic scans for examination of the sella.

NECK PAIN AND BACK PAIN

Complaints of neck pain are so often associated with headache, that in many clinical exams it is difficult to differentiate between headache and the cervical spine pain syndrome. Again, it is my assumption that a detailed history, physical and neurological exam has been done. Neuroradiological exams that are often used include:

> Plain spine radiography; Tomograms; Myelography using either oil-base contrast material, pantopaque, or water-soluble contrast material metrizamide; Discography; Epidural venography; Air myelography; Computerized tomography of the spine; and Spinal angiography.

Again, the basic issues confronting the interpreter of radiograhic studies and the referring physician are as to whether or not the patient's symptoms and neurological findings are related to any abnormalities that might be detected on the radiographic studies; and secondly, if the radiographic studies are normal, what are the chances for a false negative x-ray study.

Plain film radiographs of the spine are indicated as the first radiographic procedure when deemed indicated, as they are reasonably economical and can be used to identify a variety of conditions, i.e., congenital defects such as hemivertebrae, scoliosis or spondylolysis as well as acquired abnormalities which may be associated with chronic trauma or age, i.e., spondylosis and/or small canal syndromes of varying degree.

Patients with back pain associated with proved herniated disc lesions may have a variety of x-ray findings. These range from being completely within normal limits to having profound x-ray changes, but certain generalizations are possible. In patients with cervical disc pain syndrome it is unusual to have completely normal plain x-rays of the cervical spine, and even more unusual to have a normal myelogram. On the other hand, in the lumbosacral spine it is not unusual to have normal or near normal plain x-rays of the spine and even normal myelography, especially if the clinically determined level is at the L. 5 S. 1 interspace. This is because of the variable anatomy in the relationship of the nerves to the herniated discs. The accuracy of myelography has been improved with the addition of water-soluble contrast agents, but false negative studies still exist at the L. 5 S. 1 disc interspace. This then explains the presence of additional examinations used in these patients, such as epidural venography in which the veins are injected which lie around the dura sac and their anatomy and localization is used to diagnose herniation of disc since herniated disc material will displace the veins or obstruct their flow. Of importance is the observation that a negative epidural venography exam is considered strong evidence that herniated disc is not present. A negative myelogram at L. 4, 5 level is quite accurate but not as accurate at L. 5 S. 1. Epidural venography is more useful at this level (L. 5 S. 1).

A direct examination of the disc via discography is possible in which a contrast agent is directly injected into the disc itself via a percutaneous needle. This technique has largely been abandoned because of variable results and because of its heavy reliance upon clinical subjective patient data during the examination. This procedure has a high false positive incidence in the population over 35 years of age. Holt injected three cervical discs in each of 50 asymptomatic prison volunteers from ages 21 to 50 and found that a normal study was present in only 10 percent. This obvious high incidence of false positive has largely led to the procedure falling into disrepute. Spinal angiography is used in a very specific limited way in vascular conditions such as AV malformation in certain post-traumatic states.

Computerized tomography is being developed as a selective problem-solving technique and may prove to be more accurate than either plain film myelography or venography. Preliminary work with a prototype specialized neurological CT scanner have shown that herniated discs can be identified without the addition of contrast material such as metrizamide. At present, however, it is still used as a problem-solving technique after plain films and noncontributory or confusing myelographic or epidural venographic studies.

The importance for accurate, conscientious clinical correlation of clinical findings and abnormal radiographic findings cannot be overemphasized. Abnormal plain x-ray spine findings can be seen in up to 50 percent in patients over 50 years of age, and over 75 percent in patients over 65 years of age. McCrae in 240 patient without cervical or cord symptoms found degenerative changes at C. 5, 6 and C. 6, 7 or at the apophyseal joints, in 50 percent of patients over 40 years of age (McCrae, 1976). Therefore, if we know that a plain film findings are abnormal almost universally in the given population over 40 years of age, considerable care must be attached to positive x-ray findings. These observations may even be extended to myelographic findings. Martins found that in 144 patients ages 19 to 54 in whom myelography was done without cervical symptoms, 41 percent over age 40 had an abnormal myelogram and 62 percent over age 50 had an abnormal myelogram. These defects that were found were indistinguishable from those described in patients with symptoms that were felt to be significant (Martins et al., 1976). Although the reported overall accuracy of lumbar myelography is stated at 73 percent and that venography is 94 percent, knowledge of the aforementioned statistics is imperative since the abnormal findings may not be related to the patient's symptomatology.

In spite of these sobering statistics, following neurological consultation the following might be considered for recommendation in symptomatic patients. Neurological history, physical and examination is obviously done first. Plain films and stress films to detect subluxations and congenital anomalies might then be the first radiological exam depending upon the clinical symptomatology. Myelography would be the next step and if equivocal or negative, epidural venography would be considered in the lumbar area. The contribution of computerized tomography is not known at present, but still may be used in the small canal syndrome, in complex fractures and when myelography or epidural venography are inclusive. Often, we have used epidural venography as the first invasive technique before myelography because it has low-risk morbidity, and can be done as an outpatient procedure.

Vertigo

The final symptom complex which I will consider for neuroradiological discussion is that of vertigo or dizziness. This symptom is probably secondary only to headache in its overall incidence in complaints referable to the skull. Neuroradiological exams in the evaluation of vertigo will relate to the potential diagnosis. The following table adapted from English (with the author's permission) summarized the potential underlying diagnosis and the relative neuroradiological contribution in diseases of the vestibule (English 1976).

Vestibular Diseases	Neuroradiological Exam Contribution
Endolymphatic Hydrops	+ −
Acute Labyrinthitis	−
Vestibular Neuronitis	−
Benign Positional Vertigo	−
Acoustic Neuroma	+
PICA Syndrome (Wallenberg's Syndrome)	+
Cerebellar Tumor	+
Multiple Sclerosis	−
Cervical Vertigo	−
Arteriosclerotic Cardiovascular Disease	−
Psychoneurotic Vertigo	−
Trauma (post-traumatic vertigo)	+

A basic underlying premise is present that without objective neurosensory findings, x-ray radiological examinations will not have a contribution and the degree of confidence of diagnosis from a neuroradiological standpoint is zero. We would emphasize that the natural pattern for referral should be that the patient with a symptom complex having seen his local physician, would consult on a referral basis the otologist or ENT physician and then perhaps be referred for a variety of some specialized tests which might include neuroradiological examinations in addition to the usual otological testing procedures. Only the clinical evaluation and judgment of the examining physician determines whether or not additional radiological studies are indicated.

Time does not permit the evaluation of all of the potential causes for dizziness from a neuroradiological standpoint, but perhaps one of the most common is that of the acoustic neuroma tumor suspect.

Tinnitus or ringing in the ears and/or dizziness may be a symptom in patients with acoustic neuroma, but objective exams will demonstrate hearing loss in the majority of patients. Pressure on the superior or inferior vestibular nerve can cause unsteadiness and/or vertigo. Pressure on the cochlear nerve may cause hearing loss of tinnitis. If these lesions are large the brain stem or the seventh nerve may also be involved. A neuroradiological exam really only identifies late changes since only secondary effects are seen. It may be that brainstem evoked potential responses will be potentially able to diagnose and confirm smaller and earlier lesions and most of our attention probably should be towards identifying that earlier group of patients.

Following otological clinical exam, the neuroradiological exams used in evaluation for acoustic neuroma include: plain skull x-rays, temporal bone tomograms, Stenver views, polytome petrous pyramid tomograms, computerized tomography, pneumoencephalography, angiography, brain scan, and posterior fossa contrast material examinations.

Despite common use of skull and plain temporal bone and mastoid films and reports of their value in proven cases of acoustic neuroma, plain films or special plain view films of the skull have a less than 75 percent yield in proven cases of acoustic neuroma (Dubois et al., 1978). Reidy found a 75 percent positive abnormality in plain-film film yield in 156 proven cases of acoustic neuroma (Shapiro, 1975). The addition of sophisticated polytome x-ray examinations adds a small percentage increase in accuracy and gives additional information about the overall otologic abnormalities within the temporal bone. The x-ray tomograms gives a global view of the auditory apparatus and vestibular system including an evaluation of the middle ear tympanic cavity, ossicles, cochlear and vestibular apparatus, semi-circular canals as well as the jugular bulb and internal auditory canal. Pantopaque oily contrast cisternography has been found to yield 100 percent diagnosis in acoustic neuroma, but introduces a contrast material that cannot be totally removed. Pneumoencephalography is highly accurate but requires sophisticated polytome equipment and has moderate morbidity and expense.

Brain scans have been found to have a low yield of accuracy and require large lesions for diagnosis. Computerized tomography with the use of IV contrast material has been found to have 100 percent accuracy if these lesions are over 3 cms in size and 90 percent accuracy if the lesions is over 1½ cms in size. Amipaque or metrizamide study in the sub-arachnoid space in addition to computerized tomography has diagnosed 100 percent lesions in the small series; thus, even lesions under 1 cm. in size can be seen with computerized tomography and amipaque if overlapping slices and sophisticated CT is available (Dubois et al., 1978).

In view of this the following algorithm is proposed (Dubois et al., 1978).

Protocol For Evaluation of Acoustic Neurilemmoma

Clinical, Radiographic, or
Tomographic Abnormality

Computed Cranial Tomography
(intravenous contrast agent)

Positive	Negative
Surgery or Arteriography	Ampaque CT or Pantopaque Cisternography Cisternography

In summary, the impact of neuroradiological technique in the evaluation of symptom complexes is limited by the number of cases in whom false negatives and false positives occur. These limitations force a close critical cooperation between the referring physician, specialist and consulting neuroradiologist. A summary of the radiological exams' cost, morbidity and relative sensitivity, specificity and false positives follows [Table 1]. A summary of representative radiation exposure to the patient in various radiographic exams is demonstrated in [Table 2].

An ideal test which combines features of low cost, low morbidity, high sensitivity, high specificity, low false positives and false negatives and low radiation exposure does not exist in the laboratory or in radiology today. The closest to the ideal in our opinion is a careful history and physical exam, and a thoughtful physician/examiner who uses consulting tests critically.

Table 1

Exam	Cost	Morbidity	Sensitivity	Specificity	False −	False +
Ideal	L	L	H	H	L	L
Skull	L	L	L	L	H	L
Cervical Spine	L	L	H	L	L	H
Lumbar Spine	L	L	L	L	M	M
Polytome	M	L	H	M	L	L
C.T. Head	M	L	H	L	L	L
C.T. Spine	M	L	H	M	L	M - L?
RNS Flow	M	L	M	L	H	L
RNS Static	M	L	M	L	M	L
Myelogram	M	M	H	L	L	H
Discography	M	M	H	H	L	H
Epidural Venography	M	L	H	M	L	L
Angiography	H	M	H	M	L	L
Peg	H	H	H	M	L	L

L = Low
M = Moderate
H = High

Table 2
Radiation Dose of Various Radiological Exams

Site	Projection	Surface	Gonad Male (mrad)	Gonad Female (mrad)
Skull	Lateral	96	.04	.05
Lumbar Spine	Ap	221	15	70
	Lateral	820	9	61
	L. 5, S. 1 spot	1100	55	82
Chest	PA	9.21	.02	.04
CT (head EMI 1010)		2400	.2	.1
Radionuclide Brain Scan 10 mCi IV 99m Tcpertechnitate			120	180

REFERENCES

Duboulay, G. and Marshall, John, Comparison of EMI and Radioisotope Imaging in Neurological Disease. *Lancet,* VII, 1294–1297, December 27 (1975).

Dubois, Philly J., M.B.B.S., *et al.* An Evaluation of Current Diagnostic Radiologic Modalities in the Investigation of Acoustic Neurilemoma. *Radiology* V126, 173–179, January (1978).

English, Gerald M. *Otolaryngology.* Harper & Row, 113–114 (1976).

Fineberg, Harry V., Bauman, Rover and Sosman, Martha. Computerized Cranial Tomography; Effect on Diagnostic and Therapeutic Plan. *JAMA,* Vol. 238, No. 3, 224–227, July 18, 1977.

Kieffer, Stephen A. "The Radiographic Evaluation of Brain Tumors - A Reconsideration of Priorities," John H. Juhl Lecture, University of Wisconsin, November 16, 1979.

Martins, A.N., *et al.* Reappraisal of the Cervical Myelogram. *Journal of Neurosurgery,* Vol. 27, 27–31 (1976).

McCrae, Donald L. Asymptomatic Intervertebral Disc Protrusions. *Acta Radiology,* Vol. 46, 9 (1976).

Nadich, Thomas P., Soloman, Seymout and Leeds, Normal. Computerized Tomography in Neurological Evaluations. *JMA,* Vol. 240, No. 6, 565–568, August 11, 1978.

Reidy, J., deLacey, G.L., Wignall, B.K. and Uttley, D. The Accuracy of Plain Radiographs in the Diagnosis of Acoustic Neuromas. *Neuroradiology, Vol. 10,* 31–34 (1975).

Shapiro, Robert T. *Myelography,* 3rd Edition. Year Book Publishers, Inc., Chicago, Illinois (1975).

5
Evoked Potentials

LAVAR G. BEST

INTRODUCTION

In the last few years, there has been a marked increase in the use of evoked potentials in the workup of the clinical patient. A continuing development in technique, sophistication of equipment, and experience in the utilization of evoked potential data as an aid in the differential diagnosis of the patient have all been contributing factors. Actually, the recording of the evoked potentials as a means of evaluating neurosensory function began in the early 1960's coincident with the development of the small summing computer. At that time evoked potentials were recorded from stimuli including auditory, visual, and somatosensory and of these various sensory modalities, probably the testing of auditory function received the earliest attention.

The evoked potential, as discussed in this chapter, is a recording of a voltage field measured from the scalp and is a reflection of the aggregate of the underlying neural action potentials. Each contributing action potential is a result of a sequence of changes in the membrane ion permability along an axion. Also contributing to the evoked potential is the current generated at synaptic junctions as a result of the depolarization accompanying the excititory and inhibitory post-synaptic potentials. These action potentials, both axionic and synaptic, are only those potentials which are triggered (evoked) by a specific sensory stimulus, such as audition, vision, etc. This, then, distinguishes them from the ongoing rhythmic action potentials such as found in the electroencephalogram.

The sensory-evoked potentials are of extremely small voltage, .05 uv to 45 uv, and extremely fast with some potentials having a duration of less than 10 msec. This means that these potentials are hidden in the larger ongoing neuroelectric activity of the cerebrum or brainstem which necessitates that they be recorded by a computer system. The computer detects these small potentials by means of summing technique, wherein the evoked potential is isolated from the larger ongoing biological noise.

Each of the various sensory stimuli produce a uniquely different recorded evoked potential. The number of components within the potential, the latencies, and amplitudes of the various evoked potentials are different. However, in addition to the unique characteristic of the evoked potential in relationship to the sensory stimulus which evoked the pattern, the evoked potential changes, often times dramatically, in response to variations within a given stimulus. For example, changing the intensity or repetition rate of the auditory signal will cause quite significant changes in the appearance of the auditory evoked potential and thus the recognition of the evoked potential becomes somewhat arbitrary. So, even though the evoked potential study is considered to be "an objective test," there may be a lot of subjectivity as far as choosing the parameters of the test and also interpreting the test result.

The validity and reliability of the various evoked potential tests recorded must be established by each clinic in order to be of value in the diagnostic workup. The literature on evoked potential studies has demonstrated that there are differences in latency and amplitude of the evoked potentials which are due solely to differences in equipment and procedure in various laboratories.

In order to assure validity and reliability, one must first assess that the equipment used is capable of handling the demands placed on it by evoked potential measurements. The amplifiers must be of the best quality having characteristics of high gain, low noise and variable frequency filtering. The computer must have adequate sampling speed and storage capabilities to handle the events occurring in the accumulation of the evoked potential. The stimulus generators must have the flexibility necessary to produce the various stimuli and the necessary modifications of stimulus intensity, repetition rate, etc. Equally important in establishing validity and reliability of the evoked potential, is the qualification of the personnel conducting the test in the specific clinical setting. An understanding of the techniques of recording electrophysiological data, basic understanding of neurophysiology, and an appreciation and understanding of computer techniques in the recording of physiological data is an absolute necessity. In regard to the latter point, one cannot overstress the necessity for recognizing the limitations, as well as the possibilities, of computer analysis of data. Illustrating this point is the statement attributed to Dr. Nelson Y.S. Kiang who pointed out that the computer will accept the most mundane of preparation and print it out in a pristine form. It is hoped, eventually, that there will be a standardization of equipment and procedures so that inter-laboratory results can be more precisely compared, but until then, each individual laboratory must establish its own norms. These norms are established in the usual maner, i.e., running a group of normal subjects for each test parameter. By recording these results and then applying a statistical evaluation to the results one can establish the standard deviation of normal for latency characteristics and amplitude characteristics of the evoked potential. Once these standard deviations have been obtained, it is a matter of comparing subsequent evoked response recordings to these standard deviations to establish the normalcy or abnormality of the obtained evoked potentials. Again, there is a divergence of opinion as to the standard deviation value which best represents the normal population. Some literature reports one standard deviation, others report two standard deviations and some propose as high a standard deviation as ± 2.58 which would allow approximately 99 percent of a normal population to lie within the standard deviation limits.

TESTING SENSORY FUNCTION

Auditory function can be measured by two different techniques, one being a cortical evoked potential and the other being a brainstem evoked potential. The former is often called the slow or long latency evoked potential and is the potential which was studied early in the 1960's and received a great deal of development in the subsequent years. The potential is evoked generally by puretones of rather short duration, 300 to 500 msec, and in frequencies in octave or half-octave steps from 250 Hz to 8000 Hz. Standard earphones are the stimulus transducers. The potential is detected by an electrode array which includes an active electrode at the vertex, a reference electrode at the ipsilateral earlobe or mastoid and a ground electrode at the contralateral earlobe or mastoid area. The evoked potential is considered to be the reflection of the non-specific cortical response fields radiated from the vertex. This same electrode location provides a pickup for other sensory evoked potentials and thus it is described as a secondary or non-specific response field. Also because of its non-specific and slow response characteristics, it is very susceptible to changes of physiological state of the patient, i.e., sleep, attention, certain drugs and states of sedation or anesthesia. As the results are so readily influenced by

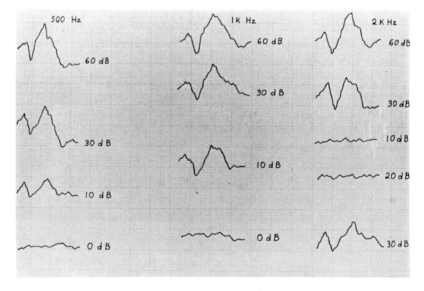

Fig. 1.   Slow auditory cortical evoked potentials used to determine threshold of response at frequencies of 500 Hz., 1kHz., and 2kHz. in the right ear.

these factors, this test is not the test of choice to be used in the auditory evaluation of an uncooperative subject who might require sedation during the examination.

[Figure 1] shows an auditory cortical evoked potential test on an individual who was indicating by subjective hearing tests a severe hearing loss with thresholds of 80 dBHL at 500 Hz and 90 dBHL at 1000 and 2000 Hz. As illustrated from Figure 1, at 500 Hz with an intensity of 60 dB, a cortical auditory evoked potential was obtained. The intensity of the stimulus was decreased to 30 dBHL, then 10 dBHL and ultimately, 0 dBHL. At 10 dBHL the response was still present. At 1000 Hz a stimulus of 60 dBHL, 30 dBHL and 10 dBHL again produced a visible evoked potential. At 2000 Hz, a 60 and 30 dBHL intensity tone produced an evoked potential, but at 10 dBHL and 20 dBHL there was no potential recorded. This, then, would indicate a threshold at 2000 Hz of between 20 and 30 dBHL. In summary, the evoked potential study showed recorded potentials at 10 dBHL at 500 Hz, 10 dBHL at 1000 Hz., and 30 dBHL at 2000 Hz or normal hearing up to 2000 Hz and then a mild loss at that frequency.

The second auditory evoked potential is referred to as a brainstem auditory evoked potential and is one of the most recent of the evoked potentials studied. This potential is often referred to as a far-field potential. By this it is meant that even though the detecting electrodes are on the scalp (vertex) the neural generators of the evoked potential are located deep to the cerebral cortex, i.e., in the brainstem. The stimuli to evoke this potential are usually square wave pulses of 100 microsecond duration given at a very rapid rate, approximately 10 to 30 per second. These impulses are fed into a earphone which produces an auditory 'click' stimulus. The electrode array for this potential is the same as that for auditory cortical potentials. Namely, an active electrode at the vertex, a reference electrode at the ipsilateral earlobe and a ground electrode at the opposite earlobe or mastoid region. The evoked potential is a short duration potential lasting approximately 10 msec for its major components and is usually identified by seven (7) major positive waves. The first wave occuring at

approximately 1.5 msec after the stimulus and each component thereafter at approximately 1 msec intervals. The evoked potential reflects the activity of the auditory neural
pathway in the brainstem with the first component wave
thought to be generated as a compound action potential of
the 8th nerve, the second component generated at the
cochlear nuclei, the third component at the superior olivary
complex, the fourth component at the lateral lemniscus, and
the fifth component generated at the inferior colliculus. The
sixth and seventh components are quite inconsistent and
often not reported. They are thought to be generated at the
area of the medial geniculate bodies and the auditory radia-
tions respectively.

In distinction to the cortical auditory evoked potential,
this latter potential, the brainstem evoked potential, is
relatively unaffected by the physiological state of the subject, i.e., sleep and drugs. This makes this test the auditory
evaluation of choice when these conditions are present.

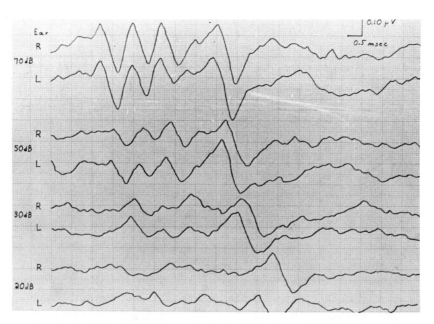

Fig. 2. Brainstem auditory evoked potentials demonstrating response to
click stimuli given in descending intensity level to a normal threshold
value.

However, there is a major limitation of the brainstem auditory evoked potential test. With the square wave stimuli the person hears the stimulus as a 'click' and the evaluation of hearing is then limited to only high frequencies with a center frequency of the click being usually between 2000 and 3000 Hz. Tests using so-called tone pips or short tone bursts which have some tonality to them in the mid and low frequencies are being used in the brainstem auditory evoked potential tests; however, at the present time, these have limitations as to their intensity range and tone pips below 1K Hz are still of questionable value for determining threshold levels.

[Figure 2] illustrates the use of the brainstem auditory evoked potential in evaluating a case reporting a unilateral hearing loss. Both right and left ear results are shown to illustrate the symmetry of findings. The patient presented at the examination with normal hearing in the one ear and a total hearing loss in the left ear. As shown in Figure 2, the evoked potential was a typical pattern at 70 dBHL and as the intensity was decreased,the pattern shows the normal changes to a point at threshold wherein only component V is visible. This pattern is duplicated in both the right and left ears. In summary, the brainstem auditory evoked potential would demonstrate a normal hearing threshold for the stimulus in both right and left ears.

The somatosensory evoked potential is a complex potential having many components to its pattern, especially if the potential is measured for durations of 300 to 400 msec. The somatosensory evoked potential is measured from an electrode placed on the scalp overlying the region of the somatosensory strip of the cortex. Again, the ground and reference electrodes are placed on earlobes or mastoid areas. The stimulus is a square wave electrical pulse of 0.1 msec duration and a current strength sufficient to cause a visable muscle twitch (6–12 u amp). In assessing the upper extremities, the median nerve at the wrist is the usual site of excitation and for the lower extremities, the common peroneal at the knee or the sural nerve at the ankle are most often used. There is still much discussion as to what segments of the somatosensory evoked potential should be studied, i.e., stimulus onset to 50 msec or the middle components 50 msec to 100 msec or the entire response up to 300 msec.

As is usually found in evoked potential studies, the early components are the most stable and resistive to emotional factors, however, in the study of the psychogenic patients, it may well be that the inclusion of the long latency components which are influenced by psychological factors would be the most advantageous components for measurements.

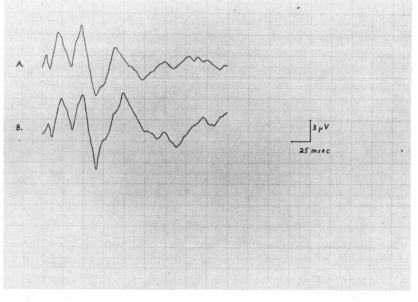

Fig. 3. Somatosensory evoked potentials obtained from median nerve stimulation. Tracing A is from right side stimulation and Tracing B is from left side stimulation.

[Figure 3] illustrates the use of the somatosensory evoked potential in the workup of a patient suspected of a functional upper extremity anesthesia. The patient was injured in a motorcycle accident and was in the process of medical-legal evaluation for compensation from that accident. The patient complained of "a lack of feeling in the hand and arm on the left side." As can be seen from the recorded evoked potentials, the somatosensory evoked potentials were equal on both sides with stimulation to the median nerve at the site of the wrist. It should be mentioned that the somatosensory evoked potential is currently thought to represent the activity of the posterior column medial lemniscus pathways. This places some limitations of interpretation as to other sensory functions such as pain and temperature.

The visual evoked potential is a very constant potential and thus has been of considerable value when used in the differential diagnosis of non-organic and organic disorders of vision. Stability of the response was not enjoyed in the early studies which used a light flash as the stimulus, but with the development of the pattern reversal visual stimulus, the potential has become a very stable recording. The usual pattern is a reversing black and white checkerboard pattern on a TV screen. The reversal time is locked to the computer for summing the visual evoked potential to the alternating black and white squares on the TV. The electrode placement is usually with the active electrode being in midline at Oz and the reference and ground electrodes again being at Cz, earlobe, or forehead.

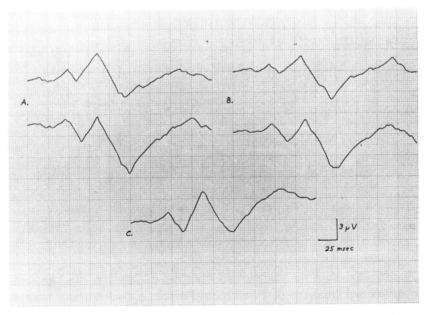

Fig. 4.   Visual evoked potentials demonstrating a normal tracing from both right eye (A) and left eye (B). Tracing (C) is a "model" normal for comparison.

[Figure 4] illustrates the visual evoked potential in a study of an individual with a history of episodes of blurred or blacked out vision and a near constant diplopia in the right eye. In comparing the visual evoked potential obtained from the patient with a model normal evoked potential, it is apparent that there is no significant difference between the two recordings. This case also illustrates a problem which may attend the measurement of the visual evoked potential and that is the uncooperative patient. In this case, the initial evoked potential recording showed a flat response which would indicate an absence of any visual stimulation. This was not considered to be a possibility in this particular situation, therefore, the test was repeated again but this time the examiner stood in front of the patient during the examination observing the reflection of the stimulus pattern on the cornea of the eye. It was observed that the patient initially tried to look away from the stimulus pattern which was probably what had occured during the first test and thus caused the absence of the response. In counseling with the patient and encouraging the patient to look directly at the stimulus, the repeated evoked potentials were within normal limits.

DISCUSSION

The text and figures of the previous sections illustrate the procedure which is used in determining the normality-abnormality, presence-absence or response to a sensory stimulus by evoked potential study. As mentioned before, it is a matter of recording the configuration of the evoked potential and comparing that to the standardized normal of the laboratory to assess whether or not the potential is within normal limits or is indeed even present. Computerized evoked potentials are generally considered to be an "objective" measure of an individuals sensory ability or threshold. This is with the understanding that the patient will provide the necessary cooperation in following the few instructions which are necessary.

For example, the patient must be physically quiet with minimal amount of movement of the body and, in some cases, the patient must attend to the stimuli in a certain manner such as in the visual evoked potential where they must look at the visual stimulus or certain segments of it. Under these conditions, the objectivity of the test is maintained because there is no subjective evaluation on the part of the patient as to their responsiveness to the stimulus. The question arises, however, about the individual who is uncooperative either because of emotional difficulty or some physical impairment which prohibits the necessary cooperation. In these situations, some corrective procedures can be used. If the individual is purposely uncooperative and the test is an auditory evoked potential study, the use of sedation is possible, particularly if the evoked potential is the auditory brainstem evoked potential. This test is shown to be resistive to changes due to behavioral states such as sedation, anesthesia, sleep, etc. The auditory cortical evoked potential can also be obtained under sedation and anesthesia; however, these physiologic states change the characteristics of the cortical auditory evoked potential. Certain corrections in values are necessary in interpreting the evoked potential under these conditions. It is obvious that if a person is uncooperative and the test is a visual evoked potential, this is difficult to handle because unlike the situation with audition where you cannot close off your ears, you can close off your visual attending to a particular stimuli and so in this particular instance, sedation is obviously of no benefit. However, a partial solution to this test limitation may be found in the use of light-emitting diodes (LED) goggles for visual stimulation. These goggles emit a light flash intense enough to be perceived thru closed eyelids yet because of their construction the flash is seen only in the eye being tested. This stimulus can then be used in those situations where the patient will not or cannot attend to the usual 'TV' type pattern-reversal visual stimulus. Normative data for this stimulus is not yet complete but should soon be available in the literature.

One of the most effective devices for correcting the problem of the uncooperative patient is to have a short counseling session with the patient previous to the test. During this session, the requirements of the test and the cooperation necessary may be pointed out. The necessity for acquiring accurate results may be stressed to the patient. Just how obvious and strong one approaches the requirements of cooperation, will vary with the rapport established with the patient and the assessment of the tester as to the effectiveness of such an approach. With an experienced tester and using good counseling techniques, it is relatively infrequent that a test cannot be accomplished because of non-cooperation from the patient from an emotional standpoint.

SUMMARY

Computerized evoked potentials are presently being used to determine the presence or absence and threshold, where appropriate, of the sensory modalities of hearing, sight and somatosenses. The evoked potentials obtained from these various sensory stimuli are considered to be an objective measure of the patient's response to the stimulus and are measured either in an all or none mode or as a threshold value. The objectivity of the evoked potential is not always absolute, however, and certain precautions must be observed.

The field of evoked potentials is still a relatively new discipline and its role in the study of the functional patient is without a large backlog of experience in many instances. However, with the continuing improvement in computers and the continuing research in neurophysiology, evoked potentials will undoubtedly provide even more information in the future in regard to the diagnosis of the functional patient.

REFERENCES

Aunon, J.I. and Contor, F.K. VEP and AEP Variability: Interlaboratory vs. Intralaboratory and Intersession vs. Intrasession Variability. *Electroenceph. Clin. Neurophysiol.*, 42, 705–708 (1977).
Bodis-Wollner, I. Recovery from Cerebral Blindness: Evoked Potential and Psychophysical Measurements. *Electroenceph. Clin. Meirpphysiol.*, 42, 178–184 (1977).

Feinsod, M., Hoyt, W.F., Wilson, W.B. and Spire, J-P. Visually Evoked Response. *Arch. Opthalmol.*, 94, 237–240 (1976).

Goldstein, R. Pseudohypacusis. *J Speech Hear. Dis.*, 31, 341–352 (1966).

Kooi, K.A., Yamada, T. and Marshall, R.E. Binocular and Monocular Visual Evoked Responses in the Differential Diagnosis of Psychogenic and Disease-Related Visual Disorder. *Interntl. J. of Neurology.*, 9, 272–286 (1975).

Levy, R. and Mushin, J. The Somatosensory Evoked Response in Patients with Hysterical Anesthesia. *J Psychosomatic Research*, 17, 81–84 (1973).

McCandless, G.A. and Best, L.G. Evoked Responses to Auditory Stimuli in Man Using a Summing Computer. *J Speech and Hearing Res.*, 7, 193–202 (1964).

Moldofsky, H. and England, R.S. Facilitation of Somatosensory Average-Evoked Potentials in Hysterical Anesthesia and Pain. *Arch. Gen. Psychiatry*, 32, 193–197 (1975).

Sohmer, H., Feinmesser, M., Bauberger-Tell, L. and Edelstein, E. Cochlear. Brainstem and Cortical Evoked Responses in Nonorganic Hearing Loss. *Ann. Otot.*, 86, 227–234 (1977).

Weber, B.A. and Folsom, R.C. Brainstem Wave V Latencies to Tone Pip Stimuli. *J. Am. Audiol Society*, 2, 182–184 (1977).

6
Differential Diagnosis in Clinical Neuropsychology

DONALD L. DUERKSEN
W. LYNN SMITH

Physicians frequently encounter patient symptoms which defy standard diagnosis and appear to present "functional" or "psychogenic" components. A patient may present a cluster of symptoms associated with a disease of known etiology but fail to show any underlying aspects of that disease. Others may show evidence of physical disease but present unusual symptoms or symptoms greatly out of proportion to the severity of the disorder. This is especially true of headache, back pain and other types of severe pain complaints. Yet another class of patients presents symptoms which the physician may be at a loss to evaluate, and here we are referring to complaints regading mental activity or subjective feelings, such as memory loss, personality change, disordered states of consciousness, dizziness and fainting spells.

Faced with these "problem patients," the physician is left with the dilemma of whether to treat the symptoms, keep searching for the underlying disorder which he feels may be present, or to forego treatment because of the functional appearance of the disorder. This can be quite frustrating to the physician who is earnestly attempting to relieve his patient's distress and it is easy for him to do too little or too much.

Clinical neuropsychology is able to offer medical practitioners unique information regarding the patient and his level of functioning which can help resolve these kinds of diagnostic dilemmas. It is able to do this because it not only objectively measures aspects of brain function at a level not accessible in the traditional neurological examination but additionally examines attributes of personality, motivation, and emotional state which often contribute to symptom formation. In addition, a clinical neuropsychological study is a painless and non-invasive procedure which does not contribute to the patient's physical distress.

NEUROPSYCHOLOGICAL TESTING

When one moves beyond the examination of the physical structure of the central nervous system to examine its integrity based on functional ability, the examiner finds he can assess function at various "levels." As the central nervous system nearly always functions as a coordinated whole, and description of levels is bound to be somewhat artificial, the concept is useful in describing differing approaches in examination.

The advantage of the traditional neurological examination lies in its comprehensive range and objectivity. Although it is strongest at the lower levels of functional organization through examination of reflexes, gross sensory and motor phenomena and integration of basic skills, it does examine a wide range of functions based on the absence or presence of certain pathological signs.

However, as one moves to the level of highly integrated skills and to the levels of perception and cognition, the abilities under examination become not only more complex, requiring statistically based assessment, but also become somewhat less objective due to the influence of other factors such as personality structure, emotional status, motivation, etc.

John McFie (1975), a neurologist turned neuropsychologist, reminds us that we by no means have a measure of "raw" brain function:

> Psychological testing is primarily an assessment of the function of the brain. It is true that this function passes through a number of filters, emotional and environmental, before it reaches its expression as a response to a test item, but the mechanism of the whole process is that of a pattern of neuronal discharges of chemical reactions.

We would add that assessment of higher-level brain functions is not only filtered, but in fact is actively modulated by other factors. For the neuropsychologist, this is the crucial starting point for differential diagnosis. Both brain function and the filters through which it is modulated must be accounted for in the test results. To do any less is to practice diagnosis by exclusion.

THE TEST BATTERY

There is no single test of "organicity." Of the wide range of cognitive and perceptual, receptive and expressive, memory and learning and other abilities associated with the highest level functions of the human brain, organic impairment can produce widely differing patterns of diffuse or localized impairment. Only by sampling a wide range of abilities through different modalities can an adequate description of the integrity of brain function be established. (Davison, 1974).

In a similar fashion, one test of personality is not enough to investigate both conscious and unconscious factors, style of response, emotional state and motivation which can contribute to symptom formation and influence the form and quality of mental functioning.

The extent to which one attempts to investigate these two inter-related areas of functioning determines the type of test battery needed. Different "schools of neuropsychology" have approached the problems of assessment with differing opinions and differing batteries. In general, we can group the different approaches into two broad categories. The first, which might be called the "experimentally based approach," has grown out of the pioneering work of Halstead, followed by Reitan, which led to the widely used Halstead-Reitan Neuropsychological tast battery. This approach utilizes a lengthy battery of highly specific tasks given to each patient, regardless of symptomotology. The battery does not include measures of personality although most using this approach add the MMPI (Minnesota Multiphasic Personality Inventory). This approach grew out of studies using a variety of tests and combinations of scores to differentiate the "brain damaged" from "normal" control groups, and aims for specific localization of brain lesions with indications of the type of lesion.

Unfortunately, as clinicians, we are not called upon to differentiate the "brain damaged" from "normal controls," but rather from the full spectrum of human behavioral disorders and personality types. It is this awareness that might best characterize the second group which could be called the "clinically based approach." This approach is likely to use a "core" battery of broader test measures, and then add further tests of specific abilities as indicated by performance on the "core" tests. Neuropsychologists using the clinical approach are more apt to include extensive personality measures. The aim of the clinical approach is also to diagnose impaired brain-function, but shows less emphasis on specific localization and more emphasis toward the inter-relationships between abilities and a picture of overall integrity and ability to function considering both strengths and weaknesses.

It is beyond the scope of this chapter to discuss exhaustively and sufficiently the many test measures available or the wide variety of test patterns which can be produced from either organic or psycho-emotional disorders. The interested reader is directed to the selected bibliography at the end of this chapter which includes references to more intensive discussion of topics we can only briefly touch on here.

Despite different theoretical backgrounds and differing test batteries, there is an overlap of tests used by the various approaches. We will introduce two of the most widely used measures of higher brain function and personality, the Wechsler Intelligence Scales and the MMPI.

WECHSLER INTELLIGENCE SCALES

The Wechsler Scales were constructed as multi-dimensional measures of intelligence and not as measures of brain function, though this application was soon appreciated. "If the contribution of the WAIS were to the diagnosis or organic brain disorder or dysfunction alone, its significance as a clinical instrument would be assured." (Allison, 1978).

Of the series of Wechsler Intelligence Scales for adults, the WAIS (Wechsler Adult Intelligence Scale) is used most frequently. The earlier Wechsler-Bellevue Form I and Form II are still used, often when a patient has gained familiarity with the WAIS and especially in test/retest situations. Each contains eleven subtests, divided into six Verbal subtests and five Performance subtests. The subtests yield individual scores in addition to the composite Verbal, Performance and Full Scale Intelligence Quotients.

The following material on the individual subtests has been drawn largely from Matarazzo (1972), McFie (1975) and Lezak (1976), as well as from our clinical experience.

The Verbal Subtests

Information

This subtest presents a series of questions tapping ones general fund of knowledge and correlates highly with overall intellectual level. As ability on this subtest relies heavily on long-term memory recall it is quite resistant to change in organic conditions. This test is often relatively lower in hysteria and the impulsive character disorders.

Comprehension

The questions presented on the Comprehension subtest require social knowledgeability, common sense judgment, problem-solving ability and abstraction. As these questions reflect "thought-out" answers as opposed to "remembered" answers they provide insights into the thinking process of the patient. The quality of the answers is useful in distinguishing between the deficient or peculiar thought processes of psychopaths or schizophrenics as compared to the confusion and lack of mental flexibility of some organic patients. This is a posterior left frontal lobe test.

Similarities

This subtest requires the patient to name a logical similarity to each of a series of pairs of increasingly divergent items. It has been considered a measure of concept formation and verbal reasoning. The subtest is relatively insensitive to personality factors in the absence of psychosis, but may show a marked deficit in cases of left temporal lobe impairment.

Arithmetic

The questions of this subtest are presented as arithmetic word-problems which the patient is required to solve without the use of pencil and paper. As such, it requires intact memory and concentration, but results vary considerably with educational and occupational background. If a poor performance on the test can be shown to be associated with an actual calculation deficit, impaired functioning of the left parietal area is indicated.

Digit Span

This subtest requires the patient to first repeat after the examiner a series of numbers of increasing length and, in the second part, to repeat the series backward from the presented order. The first part of the test is a straight forward measure of immediate memory for verbal material and a deficit here suggests impairment to the left frontal and temporal areas. A deficit on the second part while the first is intact is often seen in generalized impairment. In addition, this subtest is particularly sensitive to anxiety which can substantially reduce the score. Some depressed patients appear actually to perform relatively better on this test than would be expected from the remainder of their performance.

Vocabulary

The Vocabulary subtest is similar to the Information subtest in that it is the most highly correlated with general intellectual level and does not decline with age. Because of these features it is important in indicating the premorbid intellectual level of the patient. The subtest is also helpful in substantiating subtle dysphasias, i.e., those with difficulty in finding the "right" word. Vocabulary is a left temporal lobe test.

The Performance Subtests

Picture Completion

This subtest presents 21 incomplete pictures from which the patient is required to name what important part is missing. Like the Vocabulary and Information subtests of the Verbal scale, it is largely unaffected by intellectual changes due to the aging process of diffuse/generalized organic impairment, and is often a good measure of premorbid intellectual status. Performance on this subtest can be affected in patients with a naming disability or disordered visual recognition. Psychotic patients frequently show bizarre or inappropriate responses as opposed to the concrete or confused answers of organics.

Picture Arrangement

This subtest presents a series of eight comic-strip-like sequences of pictures, presented to the patient in mixed-up order. The patient is required to reorder the sequence to complete a sensible story. Those with lesions affecting the frontal and temporal areas of the right hemisphere often show severe deficits on this subtest, however, schizophrenics frequently show moderate difficulty as well.

Block Design

In this subtest the patient is required to construct geometric patterns using colored blocks from the designs presented on cards by the examiner. All the blocks are identical having all red, all white and half red/half white sides. Poor performance on this subtest in one of the best WAIS indicators of organic dysfunction. Some decrease in expected score is seen in nearly all organic conditions producing diffuse impairment. Increased difficulty is noted with right hemisphere impairment increasing to severe loss of performance in those with lesions in the right parietal area. This subtest does not vary greatly with differing personality types but can show deficits due to slowed execution time in depression or poor motivation and frustration in anxiety states.

Digit Symbol

This is a timed paper-and-pencil test which presents the digits 1 through 9 matched with a nonsense symbol. The patient is required to write the matching symbol below a random sequence of the digits and to do as many as possible in 90 seconds. This subtest requires visual-motor coordination and concentration. Of the WAIS battery it is one of the most sensitive to organic impairment, regardless of type or location. Like the Block Design subtest it can be affected by emotional and motivational states.

Object Assembly

The Object Assembly subtest presents four relatively simple cut-apart figures which are to be joined to complete a whole picture, much like a child's puzzle. Deficits on this subtest are usually associated with right hemisphere impairment, especially posterior quadrant. In individuals of low intellectual endowment, this subtest often shows the highest score.

WAIS PATTERNS
IN NEUROPSYCHOLOGICAL DIAGNOSIS

As mentioned previously, in addition to a single weighted score for each of the subtests discussed above, the WAIS yields separate Verbal, Performance and Full Scale I.Q. scores. Substantial differences between Verbal and Performance I.Q. is a feature often noted in patients with organic cortical dysfunction.

The subtests of the Verbal scale require the patient to attend to auditory-verbal material and to formulate a verbal response. As such, adequate performance requires intact abstract language function associated with the functioning of the left cerebral hemisphere, and patients with lateralized lesions of the left hemisphere frequently show a relative drop in Verbal Scale I.Q. However, beyond the adequate use of language functions, the Verbal scale subtests require one to attend to and remember a momentary stimulus; hence, disorders of attention-span and memory often show as relative decreases in the Verbal Scale I.Q.

Conversely, the subtests of the Performance Scale show little reliance on memory functions as the stimulus is constantly present througout each task. These subtests require motor control, coordination and speed. Deficits in these areas, often seen in cases of diffuse/generalized impairment, will produce a relatively lowered Performance Scale I.Q. even in the absence of a specific visual-spatial deficit which produces the most pronounced decrease.

In addition, the abilities required by the Verbal subtests largely draw on "old" learned material, whereas much of the Performance Scale presents relatively "novel" material. As patients with organic cortical dysfunction may show an inability to apprehend new material quickly while showing generally intact use of old or overlearned material, a decrease in the Performance Scale I.Q. may result. P.S. is sensitive to lesions on the right.

Although individual subtests scores are important, it is often the overall pattern of subtest scores which is the most revealing. A lowered subtest score must make sense with the rest of the subtests and with performance on other tests of the battery relating to the same function before it can be considered an indication of organic impairment.

One attempt to use the inter-subtest differences in scores to diagnose brain dysfunction was Wechsler's (1944) Deterioration Quotient, slightly modified by McFie (1975). The quotient contrasts those subtests least likely to decrease with age against those most likely to decrease. McFie's formula adds the scored of Vocabulary and Picture Completion, multiplied by two, to form the "Hold" score and the addition of the scores of Digit Span, Arithmetic, Block Design and Digit Symbol to form the "Don't Hold" score. The formula for the Deterioration Quotient is: Hold minus Don't Hold, divided by Hold, multiplied by 100, and scores above 20 percent have been considered suggestive of organic impairment. However, used in isolation, the Deterioration Quotient is rather poor in differentiating the brain damaged from non-brain damaged. Although normal variations in subtest scores can produce Deterioration Quotients, the greatest errors are likely to occur in cases of psychopathology and emotional disruption. However, the Deterioation Quotient is a useful index of mental efficiency whatever the underlying causative factors may be, so remains a useful addition to the clinical analysis.

THE MINNESOTA MULTIPHASIC PERSONALITY INVENTORY

The MMPI is one of the most widely used instruments of personality assessment. It is relatively easy to administer and score and has attracted investigation producing a wide body of associated research. The test consists of 566 statements which the patient must answer as true or false. The patient's responses produce scores on three validity and 10 basic clinical scales. Nine of the clinical scales and the validity scales were produced by the original work of Hathaway & McKinley (1943). One additional clinical scale, Social Introversion by Drake (1946), was added shortly after and is now considered one of the standard clinical scales. The scales were constructed by comparing the answers of criterion groups of different diagnostic categories at the University of Minnesota Hospitals to a variety to "normal" groups. The items that differentiated between the criterion groups and the normal groups at the best level were assigned to the appropriate scales (Graham, 1978). The names of the scales followed the original diagnostic criteria and today the scales are often referred to by their abbreviation or number. A short discussion of each of the scales follows, based on material from Larcher (1974) and Graham (1978).

Validity Scale "L"

Elevations on this scale indicate a person is trying to create a favorably impression by being less than honest in answering the items. It is associated with rigidity and lack of insight.

Validity Scale "F"

Extreme elevations suggest an invalid profile due to "faking bad." It is also usually elevated in severe psychopathology and in states of confusion.

Validity Scale "K"

Elevations on this scale are associated with defensiveness, inhibition and a lack of insight. Extreme scores may indicate a distorted profile due to "faking good" if high, or a lack of normal defenses if low, but within limits is an indication of the level of "neurotic" defensiveness.

Clinical Scale 1, Hypochondriasis (Hs)

Elevation on the Hs scale suggests excessive bodily concern and is associated with demanding, self-centered attitudes.

Clinical Scale 2, Depression (D)

An elevated score on the D scale is associated with feelings of depression, irritability and dissatisfaction. Individuals with the scale elevated are often pessimistic, over-controlled and lacking self-confidence.

Clinical Scale 3, Hysteria (Hy)

This scale suggests the use of conversion symptoms, correlating with Scale 1, as well as reflecting other general aspects of hysteria seen in the over-use of repression and denial. Elevation on this scale is associated with a lack of insight, and also with self-centeredness and demands for attention and affection.

Clinical Scale 4, Psychopathic Deviate (Pd)

This scale was constructed to identify those with a tendency to act-out their impulses. It is associated with asocial or antisocial behavior, low frustration tolerance, immaturity, superficial relationships and a general lack of internalized conflict, a feature that oftens helps acting-out individuals create a good first impression.

Clinical Scale 5, Masculinity/Femininity (Mf)

The Mf scale, originally constructed to attempt to identify homosexual from heterosexual men, generally reflects the degree of sterotypic sex-role identification. Elevation on this scale for men is associated with wide range of interests, passive traits, sensitivity, and good judgment. A low score for men suggests emphasis on strength and physical action and is associated with a narrow range of interests and an adventuresome, easy-going manner. Elevated scale scores for females suggests a rejection of the traditional feminine role and is associated with assertive and competitive attitudes. Low scores for females suggest the stereotypic passive role, modest traits and personality restriction.

Clinical Scale 6, Paranoia (Pa)

An elevated scale 6 indicated suspiciousness, interpersonal sensitivity and rationalizing and projecting defenses, often associated with frankly psychotic behavior. Interestingly, a very low scale 6 also indicates paranoid ideation in a more evasive and secretive individual.

Clinical Scale 7, Psychasthenia (Pt)

An elevation on this scale suggests general discomfort and is associated with anxiety, self-doubt, insecurity, guilt, as well as ineffective use of obsessive-compulsive defense mechanisms such as intellectualization, rationalization and isolation of affect. Scale 7 is the MMPI's best indicator of anxiety.

Clinical Scale 8, Schizophrenia (Sc)

An elevation on scale 8 is correlated with feelings of alienation, social withdrawal, unusual thought processes and unusual perceptions. This scale is quite poor at differentiating schizophrenics from other diagnostic categories, as many nonschizophrenics can show substantial elevations. It does, however, indicate in a general sense the level of intact ego integration versus ego decompensation.

Clinical Scale 9, Hypomania (Ma)

An elevation on scale 9 suggests a high activity level, impulsive behavior, low frustration tolerance and possibly manic excitement, agitation or grandiosity. A very low scale 9 is often helpful in diagnosing a sub-clinical depression even without substantial scale 2 (D) elevation.

Clinical Scale 0, Social Introversion (Si)

An elevated scale 0 is associated with discomfort in social situations, inhibition, lack of self-confidence and oversensitivity. High elevations suggest significant withdrawal and interpersonal anxiety.

MMPI DIAGNOSTIC PATTERNS

As is the case with the WAIS subtests discussed earlier, the entire configuration of the MMPI scales, rather than single elevations, is the most revealing. The personality and behavioral attributes indicated by a single elevated scale may be highly modified, or even substantially absent, in the presence of another elevated scale. For example, the elevated Scale 1 (Hs) suggests a great deal of concern regarding the functioning of the body. If it is present with an elevated Scale 3 (Hy) and a low Scale 2 (D), it forms the characteristic "V" often noted in cases of conversion hysteria. If found with an elevated Scale 8 (Sc), a prepsychotic state with somatic delusions is possible. If Scale 1 is elevated along the Scale 4 (Pd), the usual impulsive behavior indicated by Scale 4 is often absent, but manipulation of others through somatic complaints is often seen. If Scale 1 is elevated along with Scale 9 (Ma), somatic complaints are present along with hyperactivity and denial of disability, a self-contradictory pattern which is sometimes noted in those with organic brain dysfunction.

In the diagnosis of functional disorders, it is Scales 1 and 3 which are the most important, forming the conversion "V" mentioned above. However, because of the modifying effect of the other scales, the pattern is not always a valid indicator of the strength of conversion symptoms. As we have been called upon to predict the outcome of surgery aimed at pain relief in those whose symptoms appear to have some functional basis, we have had considerable interest in the use of the MMPI to assess the functional component of symptom complaints. This interest led us to the development of the Pain Assessment Index (Smith & Duerksen, 1980) which is based on the elevations of scales

1 and 3, but modified by scales 2, 7, and 9. In our preliminary study the index correctly identified 29 of 31 surgical patients in terms of whether they would or would not experience significant pain relief following surgery.

Overall, the MMPI is a very useful measure of emotional and personality features. However, it does have its limitations and by no means offers a complete assessment of personality. Because the format of the MMPI is that of a self-report questionnaire, the patient's perception of himself in terms of symptoms, likes and dislikes, and beliefs and atti tudes toward other people and activities, is what is being measured. The perceptions of the patients may or may not be very realistic. Also, the degree to which the patient is willing to share his perceptions honestly with us can be a limiting factor. In addition, because the MMPI classifies a patient according to his similarities to criterion groups of various psychopathological states, it does not provide for much in the way of creative and individualistic aspects of personality. Other tests, particularly projective measures such as the Rorschach, must be used to tap these dimensions.

OTHER FREQUENTLY USED TESTS

The two test measures discussed above, the WAIS and the MMPI, provide a great deal of information regarding the integrity or higher cortical brain function and the personality of the patient. They do not constitute a complete neuropsychological test battery. Other tests are necessary, to measure aspects of functioning not covered by these two, and to back-up the findings by measuring the same function or trait through a different type of test and perhaps a different sensory modality.

We do not have the space to fully discuss the array of other tests used in assessing brain function and personality, but we will briefly mention a few of the more frequently used measures seen in neuropsychological assessment.

In the assessment of organic brain dysfunction, the following tests are frequently used: Halstead/Wepman Aphasia Acreening Test, Reitan/Klove Sensory Perceptual

Examination, Bender Visual-Motor Gestalt, Hanfmann-Kasanin Concept Formation Test, Memory-for-Designs, Raven Progressive Matrices, Seashore Rhythm Test, Street Gestalt Completion Test, Tactual Performance Test, Trail Making Test and the Wechsler Memory Scales.

In the assessment of personality, the following tests are used frequently: Rorschach Inkblot Projective Technique, House-Tree-Person Projective Drawings, Interpersonal Check-List, Thematic Apperception Test, and a variety of specific self-report questionnaires.

CLINICAL ASPECTS
OF NEUROPSYCHOLOGICAL ASSESSMENT

Neuropsychological testing is more than just the administration of tests and the derivation of scores, ratios and derivatives. These are quite valuable in that they provide quantifiable aspects of behavior and functioning, but the quality of behavior and of abilities is equally as important for an accurate diagnosis. Through the taking of personal information, discussion of the problem and its history in the interview, and through the quality of behavior and abilities throughout the testing sessions, one gains a sense for the patient as a unique person. It is this that gives meaning to the formal scores of the various tests measures.

Although the testing is done on both an inpatient and outpatient basis, most studies are done in a hospital setting and being a patient in a hospital is not regarded as the most pleasant of experiences. Being sick or having something "wrong with you" in itself modifies usual ongoing behavior and many patients react quite individually, often with anxiety, depression or guilt. The person as a patient suffers role change through giving up autonomy and facing forced dependency which can lead to problems with trust and feelings of alienation as well as identity diffusion. These are important factors which can influence the outcome of neuropsychological tests, and, if not properly accounted for, lead to erroneous results, incorrect diagnosis and to the even more serious consequence of the wrong treatment.

There are, additionally, patients with "la belle indifference," smiling depression or massive denial, and although these reactions are not so detrimental to the test outcome, they still offer important clues to the examiner.

Also important are the numerous and varied test expectations on the part of the patient. Some patients feel that testing is demeaning and that they may be regarded as "crazy" by the referring doctor, that their somatic complaints originate "in their heads." Some confuse neuropsychological testing with invasive procedures and develop anxiety about the potential discomfort that may be involved. Perhaps the single most frequent expectation is that, as in other diagnostic procedures, the patient will play a passive role, as in clinical laboratory studies where some sort of specimen is to be secured or a procedure is to be done while the patient lies still. In neuropsychological testing the patient is required to be an active participant from the very start. The way in which the patient approaches this testing situation is an opportunity for many behavioral nuances to be observed by the alert examiner.

In dealing with patients who have difficulty with specific tasks and items it is most important to determine whether the individual patient is truly "unable" or "unwilling" to perform various tasks. Passive resistance can be quite subtle and formidable; basic distrust is another difficult presenting problem. Cases involving litigation and eventual financial reward require the examiner to be alert to facilitative distortions. The motivation artifact is often clarified by introducing seemingly different tasks which in reality tap the same neuroanatomical/behavioral correlative areas. This can help clarify areas of cortical dysfunction or help expose the patient who is playing games with the tests.

In cases of suspected distortion, retesting at a later date with the same test will give the examiner a good basis for explaining disability. Some changes which occur in test scores can be evaluated in terms of environmental or behavioral shifts, but in general similar patterns in test/retest profiles are to be expected.

Fatigue is an important consideration. Although we can't eliminate fatigue, we can distribute it. Expecially in assessing the elderly, fatigue in the testing sessions can be controlled by using shortened sessions spread out over several periods. The elderly often do better in the mornings and multiple sessions at the same time of the day are often helpful in evaluating the patient's true capabilities. It is important not to follow other anxiety-producing diagnostic procedures. In persons with seizure disorders, testing is usually discontinued after an episode once post-ictal confusion is verified. However, attempting continued testing in cases of suspected emotionally caused seizures can provide valuable diagnostic clues if significant post-ictal confusion is absent.

Not all examiners are perfect in the eyes of the patient. Often patients respond better to a female as opposed to a male examiner, or to someone older than themselves. Teenagers usually relate better to the younger clinician, while the elderly seem generally to relate better to the examiner of later maturity.

Referral-source bias is not a direct factor in the testing situation itself, but is a useful bit of awareness the examiner can put to good use for initial approaches to the examination. Most everyone has some blind spots in his personality, and this is true for the physician as well. At the same time, some physicians are astutely aware of conversion disorders, psychophysiological reactions and body delusions, and the examiner often finds test results corroborating these suspicions at a high rate of reliability.

There is considerable overlap in the test score variations and behavior between those with organic brain dysfunction and those with psychoemotional disorders. It is only through the use of both valid and reliable tests of brain function and personality and the clinical awareness of the quality of functioning that an adequate understanding of the patient and his symptoms can be provided.

CASE STUDIES

The following three case studies taken from the files of the Cortical Function Laboratory illustrate the process of neuropsychological diagnosis as it has been discussed above

Personal information and non-diagnostic features of the patients have been altered. The scores from the WAIS and the MMPI will be emphasized, although some others will be mentioned.

Case No. 1, Suspected Multiple Sclerosis

Mrs. F, a housewife in her thirties, was referred for testing because of increasingly poor coordination, weakness, visual difficulties and lapses of consciousness. Mrs. F was brought to the laboratory on a stretcher being unable to walk on her own. Several striking observations were made during the initial interview. She was quite cheerful and appeared to show an "indifference" to the severity of her disability. Her friendliness extended to the point of being somewhat flirtatious, which carried a hysterical flavor. The extreme weakness and incoordination of her arms, which would prevent her from doing well on several of the perceptual-motor tasks to follow, had evidently not prevented her from having perfectly applied makeup. These clinical features had led her neurologist to suspect a hysterical component to her disability.

Test Results

Wechsler Adult Intelligence Scale

Information	14	Digit Symbol	5
Comprehension	10	Picture Completion	9
Arithmetic	7	Block Design	11
Similarities	12	Picture Arrangement	12
Digit Span	6	Object Assembly	9
Vocabulary	13		

Verbal I.Q.	98
Performance I.Q.	95
Full Scale I.Q.	97

Deterioration Quotient 34 percent

MMPI Elevated Scales:

```
   *    *    *    *         *    *    *
Hs(1)  D(2)  Hy(3)  Pd(4)  Mf(5)  Pa(6)  Pt(7)  Sc(8)  Ma(9)
```

Other Tests

Other perceptual tests showed no impairment and in fact were done quite well. The Rorschach showed none of the impoverishment or perplexity associated with organic impairment, but rather was highly thematic and suggested considerable personality upheaval with indications of victimization as well as anxiety and hysterical personality features.

Conclusions

At first glance, the subtest variations of the WAIS appear quite dramatic. However, our clinical impression of less than ideal motivation makes the level of disability suspect. Her low scores on the Arithmetic and Digit Span subtests are consistent with anxiety and hysterical personality features. In spite of this, the pattern does not quite make sense for an organic record. If her poor coordination and weakness caused a poor score on Digit Symbol, what allowed her to do better than average on Block Design, a test requiring coordination and speed and which is sensitive to organic impairment? In addition, there is no significant Verbal/Performance difference.

The MMPI shows the characteristic "V" of conversion hysteria as well as several other elevated scales attesting to her personality upheaval.

In addition, the other test results were consistent with a psychoemotional induced disorder.

Results

Psychiatric referral was recommended and Mrs. F followed through with psychotherapy. Within six months, she had regained use of her arms and legs, though at the sacrifice of her marriage.

Case No. 2, Depression

Mr. E was a distinguished-appearing married man in his sixties. His work performance had become progressively worse over the preceding few years and the clinic physician of the large company for which he worked finally referred him to a psychiatrist because of Mr. E's reported depression. The psychiatric consultation led to hospitalization. As he failed to respond to anti-depressant medication a series of ECT treatments was instituted. Following his discharge his condition continued to deteriorate and after a few months he was admitted to a different hospital for re-evaluation. The psychiatric examination and history left some doubts as to his current status and neuropsychological testing was ordered. Mr. E was cooperative and diligent during the sessions, but was rather slow and appeared to fatigue easily. An interesting fact that emerged during the interview was that Mr. E had been quite skilled at wood-working and furniture making which he pursued as a hobby. He had, however, found himself confused and unable to continue and had stopped about a year before his hospitalization.

Test Results

Wechsler Bellevue Intelligence Scale, Form II

Information	8	Digit Symbol	7
Comprehension	13	Picture Completion	8
Digit Span	6	Block Design	5
Arithmetic	6	Picture Arrangement	8
Similarities	8	Object Assembly	-
Vocabulary	12		

Verbal I.Q.	99
Perfomance I.Q.	106
Full Scale I.Q.	102

Deterioration Quotient 40 percent

MMPI Elevated Scales:

```
    *     *     *                    *
Hs(1)  D(2)  Hy(3)  Pd(4)  Mf(5)  Pa(6)  Pt(7)  Sc(8)  Ma(9)
```

Other Tests

Other tests administered showed mixed results. The Raven Matrices were low, but the Street Gestalt Completion was done adequately, as was the Aphasia Screening Test. The Rorschach confirmed his depressed affect but also showed perceptual impotency, a feature often noted with organic records.

Conclusions

These results are highly suggestive of organic brain dysfunction. In spite of Mr. E's good motivation, a high degree of test scatter is present as well as a substantial Deterioration Quotient. The lowered subtest scores make sense in terms of a diffuse/generalized impairment showing decreases in both Verbal and Performance items sensitive to organic dysfunction. The other tests are consistent with these indications, especially the low Raven score and impoverished Rorschach. His depression, of moderate to severe proportions, was felt to be at least a partial reaction to his impairment.

Results

These findings led to further neurological study and diagnostic procedures. A CAT Scan documented mild cerebral atrophy and a RISA Scan established his low-pressure hydrocephalus. Neurosurgery for placement of a ventricular-peritoneal shunt was successful and within a year Mr. E had resumed his hobby. At last report he had completed five pieces of furniture.

Case No. 3, Head Injury

Mrs. W, a married woman in her late twenties, was in the process of recovering from a closed head injury suffered in an automobile accident about six weeks prior to her testing. Following the accident she showed confusion, visual difficulties, problems with memory and concentration and a lack of coordination. Recently she had become unable to talk except for an occasional word or two. A Speech and Hearing evaluation had indicated that complete language retraining might be necessary. Clinically she appeared emotionally labile, crying easily or suddenly becoming angry and irritable. During the testing, she was frustrated easily, especially when trying to talk. All of the Verbal measures that could be administered were answered by Mrs. W in writing.

Test Results

Wechsler Adult Intelligence Scale

Information	--	Digit Symbol	7
Comprehension	--	Picture Completion	8
Arithmetic	7	Block Design	7
Similarities	14	Picture Arrangement	10
Digit Span	11	Object Assembly	--
Vocabulary	14		

Verbal I.Q.	108
Performance I.Q.	88
Full Scale I.Q.	99

Deterioration Quotient 27 percent

MMPI Elevated Scales:

*   *   *

Hs(1)   D(2)   Hy(3)   Pd(4)   Mf(5)   Pa(6)   Pt(7)   Sc(8)   Ma(9)

Other Tests

Nearly all the other perceptual measures were at borderline levels, consistent with the WAIS and substantiating her visual-spatial difficulties. Tests of memory were generally poor. The Rorschach was also consistent with organic dysfunction appearing short and imporverished. However, the tests results did suggest additionally a high degree of anxiety and strong conflicts regarding the expression of hostility covered by generally passive and dependent traits, consistent with the MMPI scale elevations.

Conclusions

Overall, this record is certainly one of organic quality as seen in the relatively low Performance Scale I.Q., the Deterioration Quotient and the Rorschach, as well as several of the back-up test measures. However, her recent aphasic symptoms did not appear to make much sense in light of her overall test performance which showed primarily visual-spatial perceptual deficits. This feature combined with the findings of the personality measures and clinical impressions of her repressed anger led us to suspect that her aphasic symptoms had a considerable psychoemotional component. This appeared confirmed when her neurosurgeon, against our better judgment, gave her a copy of our report to read. The report made her quite angry, and, directing her anger at us, she was able to speak without difficulty. As long as she was willing to express her feelings of anger she remained able to speak.

Results

Although no one involved doubted the organic basis for most of her symptoms, the psychoemotional overlay was so great that she was transferred to the psychiatric unit to complete her recovery and to work through the blocked anger which had been inhibiting her speech. Her other symptoms began to clear slowly with increased recovery time.

SUMMARY

In this chapter, we have tried to lay the groundwork from which to understand the basic principles of neuropsychology and its contribution to differential diagnostic problems. Neuropsychological testing can provide unique information regarding the integrity of brain function which is not available from other diagnostic procedures. We have attempted to show that the personality features of the patient are not only important artifacts in the testing of brain dysfunction, but that they also are of prime importance in documenting psychoemotionally induced symptoms.

The following chapters by Professor Merskey and Dr. Rewey will elaborate on the history of our understanding of hysterical and other psychophysiological disorders and give some insight into the psychodynamic meaning of symptom formation and its treatment.

REFERENCES

Allison, Joel. Clinical Contributions of the Wechsler Adult Intelligence Scale, in *Clinical Diagnosis of Mental Disorders: A Handbook.* Wolman, Benjamin B., ed. Plenum Press, New York (1978).

Davison, Leslie A. Introduction, in *Clinical Neuropsychology: Current Status and Applications,* Reitan Ralph M. and Davison, Leslie A., eds. V. H. Winston & Sons, Washington D. C. (1974).

Drake, L. E. Scale (0) (Social Introversion), in *Basic Readings on the MMPI in Psychology and Medicine,* Welsh, George Schlager and Dahlstrom, W. Gant, eds. University of Minnesota Press, Minneapolis (1956).

Graham, John R. The Minnesota Multiplasic Personality Inventory (MMPI), in *Clinical Diagnosis of Mental Disorders: A Handbook,* Wolman, Benjamin B., ed. Plenum Press, New York (1943).

Hathaway, S. R. and McKinley, J. C. *Minnesota Multiphasic Personality Inventory: Manual.* The Psychological Corporation, New York, (1943).

Larchar, David. *The MMPI: Clinical Assessment and Automated Interpretation.* Western Psychological Services, Los Angeles (1974).

Lezak, Muriel D. *Neuropsychological Assessment.* Oxford University Press, New York (1976).

Matarazzo, Joseph D. *Wechsler's Measurement and Appraisal of Adult Intelligence.* Williams & Wilkins Company, Baltimore (1972).

McFie, John. *Assessment of Organic Intellectual Impairment.* Academic Press, London (1975).

Smith, W. Lynn and Duerksen, Donald L. Personality and the Relief of Chronic Pain: Predicting Surgical Outcome, in *Pain: Meaning & Management,* Smith, W. Lynn, Merskey, Harold and Gross, Steven C., eds. Spectrum Publications, New York (1980).

Wechsler, David. *The Measurement of Adult Intelligence.* Williams & Wilkins Company, Baltimore (1944).

BIBLIOGRAPHY

Assessment of Brain Damage: A Neuropsychological Key Approach, Russell, Elbert W.; Neuringer, Charles and Goldstein, Gerald. John Wiley & Sons, New York (1970).

Assessment of Organic Intellectual Impairment. McFie, John. Academic Press, London (1975).

Asymmetrical Function of the Brain. Kinsbourne, Marcel, ed. Cambridge University Press, Cambridge (1978).

Brain and Intelligence: A Quantitative Study of the Frontal Lobes. Halstead, Ward C. University of Chicago Press, Chicago (1947).

Clinical Diagnosis of Mental Disorders: A Handbook. Wolman, Benjamin B., ed. Plenum Press, New York (1978).

Clinical Neuropsychology: Current Status and Applications. Reitan, Ralph M. and Davison, Leslie A., eds. V. H. Winston & Sons, Washington D. C. (1974).

Diagnosis and Rehabilitation in Clinical Neuropsychology. Golden, Charles J. Charles C. Thomas Publisher, Springfield (1978).

Hemispheric Disconnection and Cerebral Function. Kinsbourne, Marcel and Smith, W. Lynn, eds. Charles C. Thomas Publisher, Springfield (1974).

Human Neuropsychology. Hecan, Henri and Albert, Martin L. John Wiley & Sons Inc., New York (1978).

Neuropsychodiagnosis in Psychotherapy. Small, Leonard. Brunner/Mazel Inc., New York (1973).

Neuropsychological Assessment. Lezak, Muriel D. Oxford University Press, New York (1976).

Neuropsychological Testing in Organic Brain Dysfunction. Smith, W. Lynn and Philippus, Marion John, eds. Charles C. Thomas Publisher, Springfield (1969).

Psychological Techniques in Neurological Diagnosis. Burgemeister, Bessie B. Hoeber Medical Division, Harper & Row Publishers Inc., New York (1962).

7
The Psychiatry of Hysterical Symptoms

H. MERSKEY

"Placed by force of circumstances at the head of a clinical unit which had an established tradition for managing those with hysterical conditions, I felt that I should, to relieve my conscience, devote my attention to this condition, towards which my taste in science carried me very little. Treating these patients, whom all authors regarded as typical of instability, irregularity, fantasy, unpredictability...gave me the utmost repugnancy. So I resigned myself and applied myself to this work."

P. Briquet, 1859, Trans. F. Mai (Mai and Merskey, 1979)

Hysteria is a curiously uncomfortable disorder for the physician, and the more the patient appears devoted to the symptom the less the physician appreciates being involved. Briquet made a sustained epidemiological study of 430 patients with hysteria. His comments above demonstrate very well the uneasiness which hysteria arouses in doctors. He himself thought that he was treating an organic disturbance of the brain. Usually today, we consider that hysteria is a psychological disorder simulating physical disease. This gives rise to anxiety, and sometimes anger, in the physician who may feel that he is, whether deliberately or otherwise, being tricked into recognizing a fradulent claim as honest illness.

The ambivalence of physicians in regard to such patients is easy to understand. There is a wish to help, and to function as a medical practitioner should. At the same time there is a suspicion or justified fear, that the complaint of a physical disorder will mislead the physician and make him look foolish, whilst the unspoken motives of the patient will produce a troublesome situation in which the physician will be manipulated and embarrassed.

Small wonder that, of all psychiatric patients, those with presumed hysterical complaints are most rejected by physicians. Yet they also provide one of the strongest reasons for psychotherapy to be a medical field of work. Traditionally, it is from the relationship with such patients that psychotherapy has developed, and medical skills provide an essential basis for the management of hysterical complaints. Insight is helpful to the physician as well as to the patient and the psychiatry of somatic symptoms commences best with the recognition of these problems. Once they are recognized they can acquire an instrumental value. They become, in themselves, a topic for assessment and research into human feeling. When that happens, we acquire a new viewpoint which allows us to approach the subject with interest and relative ease. We can begin to look for the defining features of the condition, separate it from other psychological disorders as well as physical complaints, and develop an approach to its management.

HYSTERICAL VERSUS PSYCHOSOMATIC

Emotional disturbances may cause several types of physical complaints. Schizophrenia can lead to hallucinations of bodily change. Anxiety causes a variety of effects, such as tremor and palpitations, mediated through the sympathetic nervous system. The former are normally associated with other evidence of psychosis. The latter, in simple form, are easily recognized. At times however, psychosomatic symptoms are confused with hysterical ones. The distinction is not always easy in practice but the theoretical principles involved are elegant and easy to appreciate. Unfortunately, they have been blurred and muddled by some writers and the literature on the topic is often needlessly confusing.

Psychosomatic symptoms are mainly understood to arise because emotional disturbance causes overactivity, involuntarily, in the autonomic nervous system; or else an emotional state produces behavior which inadvertently results in some physicial change. The first case is illustrated by palpitations from an increased heart rate in consequence of fear or apprehension. In this example autonomic discharges are assumed to be directly determined by the state of the hypothalamus and the limbic system. They are diffuse and non-specific. [Some autonomic responses may be voluntarily conditioned but to a lesser extent that has lately been thought (Miller, 1974).]

By contrast hysterical symptoms have three related characteristics which separate them from psychosomatic ones. First, they correspond to the patient's idea of a symptom. Secondly, they use nervous system mechanisms concerned with the voluntary innervation of a part, and thirdly, they do not correspond with the patterns of disturbance which arise when there is a lesion affecting nervous pathways. Typically the enormous damage of a brachial plexus lesion still leaves some motor power and sensation in the arm; but a hysterical paralysis of an arm, with or without anesthesia, involves a body region irrespective of segmental nervous system supply. The anesthesia terminates at the shoulder, while the paralysis extends to the muscles of the shoulder girdle. These aspects are of course dealt with more fully in previous chapters.

Hard cases naturally exist. The pain of "tension-headache" may be powered by excess contraction of scalp muscles in consequence of anxiety. An identically worded complaint can and perhaps often does occur because of hysterical mechanisms (Ludwig, 1972; Merskey, 1979) but the theoretical distinction is plain. For reasons which will be discussed next, it is best to define conversion hysteria in terms of the above characteristics. It is however obligatory, in every supposed case, to look for evidence of unconscious conflict promoting the symptom. Some authors approach the topic of conversion hysteria by defining it first of all as the production of somatic symptoms in order to relieve a conflict. This is not entirely satisfactory even with isolated conversion symptoms because some cases are found which, despite careful inquiry, do not give evidence of such conflict (Whitlock, 1967; Merskey and

Buhrich, 1975). Still more often the type of case called Briquet's syndrome (Guze, 1970) involves no current conflicts and it has to be assumed that there are lifelong buried conflicts which are never found, but on which the symptoms are based. These situations are probably more common than those in which there is some uncertainty as to whether the symptom does correspond to an idea, or can be clearly shown not to be due to an organic lesion in nerve pathways. It is better to take for the defining characteristics those events which can be more reliably discriminated. It is also more helpful in practice to use empirical criteria in place of conceptual ones. For these reasons the hysterical symptom is best defined in terms of its tendencies to accord with the patient's idea and to avoid neuroanatomical neurophysiological rules for lesions. But it is best explained and understood in terms of the conflict hypothesis.

It follows that the diagnosis of hysterical conversion is primarily made by the techniques of physical examination. Commonly this examination comes within the special field of neurology, although the general physician, internist or psychiatrist may undertake it in some instances. The treatment afterwards is essentially psychological, whether undertaken by psychiatrists or others.

In concluding this section it is unfortunately necessary to say again that hysteria and psychosomatic complaints have been needlessly confused in some places. For example, Alexander (Alexander, 1963) wrote: "Physiologically, conversion is no different from any normal innervation by which we express emotions, such as weeping, laughing or blushing or from voluntary behavior.... Repression inhibits action, and since the tension caused by the unconscious tendency cannot be relieved it becomes a chronic innervation." This confuses a psychological disposition or tendency with a physical state of the nervous system. Although conversion was originally thought of by Freud (Freud et al., 1955) as representing a change of psychic energy into a somatic state, it is now more logically regarded as a result of thought-processes which solve a conflict. To imply that a conversion system which solves a problem and perhaps also has a symbolic function is due to physical changes is unjustified logically.

DISSOCIATIVE SYMPTOMS

This discussion so far has been concerned with bodily symptoms. There are other symptoms, especially fugues and loss of memory, which are similar to conversion symptoms but which relate only to psychological complaints. These are known by convention as Dissociative Symptoms, the term indicating that there is a split in awareness between the feelings or conflict which have caused the symptoms and the symptoms itself. All conversion symptoms by this definition are dissociative, but not all dissociative symptoms are conversion ones. Some writers indicate that the term dissociation means that consciousness is altered, in other words, that some part of it is restricted or limited. I do not think that this is a generally accepted usage. Whatever the most correct view may be, both meanings of the term dissociative are in use. Strictly speaking both conversion and dissociation imply a theory for the symptom and it is probably more sound to speak of hysterical symptoms than either conversion or dissociative symptoms. In practice, all three terms are regularly used. The draft guidelines of the Diagnostic and Statistical Manual of the American Psychiatric Association (DSM-III, 1978) employ the terms somatization disorder (Briquet's syndrome), conversion disorder, psychalgia and a typical somatoform disorder all under the heading of somatoform disorders, and the terms psychogenic amnesia, psychogenic fugue, multiple personality, depersonalization disorder under the terms dissociative disorders. And the word hysteria is lost. However, conversion disorders, dissociative disorders and hysterical disorders all remain terms in widespread use.

THE RANGE OF HYSTERICAL SYMPTOMS

The range of hysterical symptoms takes in almost the whole of medicine. Any type of physical or emotional change may be utilized as a complaint to solve an emotional problem. Even such entirely physical manifestations as jaundice can (theoretically) be employed to solve conflicts, the patient for example, unconsciously focussing an excessive concern upon the symptom in order to avoid dealing with some emotional conflict. In practice the classical hysterical symptoms or fits, paralyses, anesthesias, deafness and blindness are now rare except in unsophisticated communities and in certain specialist settings like neurological clinics and orthopaedic services dealing with compensation or with pain. The latter which is a classical hysterical disorder (Merskey 1979a). Patients who may be using symptoms as a solution to conflict are liable now to speak of "depression, fatigue, pain, dizziness" and so forth rather than to present with astasia-abasia or sudden loss of sight.

In general isolated hysterical symptoms represent an acute conflict. More widespread symptoms are usually presented by patients who inhabit internal medicine clinics, surgical departments, etc. These patients tend to accumulate thick folders and from time to time physicians report the weight of their charts. Anything less than 5 kg represents a poor specimen.

The extreme range of variation amongst these patients has been captured at one end by Guze and his colleagues at St. Louis, Missouri, who define hysteria as characterized by the occurrence of a dramatic or complicated medical history beginning before the age of 35 and by the patient admitting to at least twenty-five symptoms from nine or ten special groups, e.g., headaches, paralyses, weakness, breathing difficulty, alimentary tract complaints, menstrual complaints, sexual difficulties, back or other pain and nervousness. No other disorder should be present to account for complaint (Woodruff, 1968). Later this pattern of illness was called Briquet's syndrome (Guze, 1970). It has been shown to change scarcely at all with time in affected individuals. Briquet's syndrome does not correspond to any pattern which Briquet isolated specifically (Chertok, 1975; Mai and Merskey, 1979) and represents an arbitrary separation of one end of a continuum of cases from the rest. However the work of the St. Louis group has effectively demonstrated the persistence of this pattern and its demographic and epidemiological associations including a link with sociopathic behavior in male relatives. (Cloninger and Guze, 1970). It serves to emphasize that there is a very wide range of hysterical complaints from transitory mono-symptomatic ones to multiple ones as well as a polymorphous pattern with grossly hypochondriacal features. All this comes within the spectrum of traditional hysterical symptomatology.

Further groups or conditions which have been thought to be related in some way to hysteria range from malingering through Munchausen's syndrome, Deliberate Disability, Anorexia Nervosa, Ganser's syndrome and certain types of psychosis. One general theme which leads to this grouping is that all the cases involve some type of conflict-solving by regression to more primitive modes of behavior. Regression is usually, although not always, active in the production of symptoms. [Hysterical Psychoses are an exception since repression is reduced in them, (Hirsch and Hollender, 1969)].

The personality features often overlap with those found in Briquet's syndrome or in the traditional hysterical personality type which is considered next. The psychodynamic disturbance seems to have something in common throughout the whole spectrum of these complaints and conditions. Accordingly, it is reasonable to relate them to each other and see them as varieties of a fundamental problem in personality or adjustment, often triggered by environmental stresses or difficult situations, but sharing an underlying unity in the purpose and direction of the patient's responses.

Hysterical Personality

Traditionally patients with hysterical conversion symptoms have been regarded as emotionally shallow, labile and dependent, immature, suggestible, manipulative and histrionic. They have also been thought of as more outgoing and extroverted than others and at the same time less well-adjusted sexually. Important elements of this pattern were observed by Briquet (Briquet, 1859) and were brilliantly described by Kraepelin (Kraepelin, 1904). The development of this concept of the hysterical personality has not, to my knowledge, been traced more precisely in the clinical literature although much of it is evident in the French nineteenth-century writings on hysteria, and in the behavior elicited from Charcot's patients (Charcot, 1889). Gowers (Gowers, 1893) wrote about "the physiological preponderance of emotion in females...which may be perverted either by congenital tendency or injudicious training. License and indulgence in childhood beget self-indulgence in later life.... The near relatives of the hysterical are often conspicuously deficient in judgment, and the little common sense they possess is often rendered useless by their affection for the sufferer." Men with hysteria were more likely in his view to be effeminate. In current terms the patient has a personality disorder and troubles in relationships within the family. Janet (Janet, 1894) specifically described the emotional characteristics of lability, dramatic behavior etc.; and most authors seem to take their version of the hysterical personality from him. Elaborate personality pictures are described (e.g., Lewis, 1950). De Alarcon (De Alarcon, 1973) showed that this concept of the hysterical personality persisted despite some justified criticisms by Chodoff and Lyons (Chodoff and Lyons, 1958) of the tendency to identify conversion symptoms with hysterical personality.

The latter authors demonstrated that only three out of seventeen patients with conversion symptoms had hysterical personality characteristics. In a series of 381 patients (245 F, 135 M) with conversion symptoms, Ljungberg (Ljungberg, 1957) found that 47 percent of the females and 45 percent of the males had abnormal personalities of types which would correspond mostly in North American terms to hysteria and passive-immature-dependent. His categories were hysteria, psychoinfantile and asthenic. It appears that the hysterical personality is not uniformly found with conversion symptoms. Each may occur without the other. However a significantly increased incidence of hysterical personality and passive-dependent traits is found in patients with conversion symptoms compared with other psychiatric patients without them (Merskey and Trimble, 1979). Thus there is warrant for the traditional identification of certain personality features with hysteria.

The dynamics of hysteria were or course explained by Freud (Freud, 1955) in terms of repressed sexual conflict. Freud's outstanding contribution was qualified by the experience of the Second World War in which it was shown that large numbers of previously normal men developed hysterical symptoms in the face of overwhelming dangers. It appeared unnecessary to explain all these cases purely in terms of sexual conflict (Merskey and Buhrich, 1975). However the explanation of hysterical conversion symptoms in terms of repressed conflict remains valid. In addition, it has been shown (Merskey and Trimble, 1979) that patients with conversion symptoms have more evidence of sexual maladjustment than other psychiatric patients. Later writers (Marmor, 1953; Lazare, 1971) have related hysteria to conflicts in oral development as well as in the genital sphere and their views are, in general, very relevant to the personality disorders which are called hysteria as well as to the special syndromes (Ganser's syndrome, Deliberate Disability, etc.) which nearly always occur in individuals with a personal history and characteristics marked by immaturity, dependence and childhood misfortune. The persisting theme of certain personality connotations of hysteria is thus reinforced. In a valuable brief discussion of the hysterical personality Horowitz (Horowitz, 1977), basing himself on Shapiro (Shapiro, 1965), has amplified the short-terms and long-term phenomena identifiable in this personaltiy structure. He emphasizes that the hysterical personality overall has short-, medium- and long-term personality patterns. They are described as follows:

Long-order patterns influence interpersonal relationships which are repetitive, impulsive and often characterized by victim-aggressor, child-parent, and rescue or rape themes. "Cardboard" fantasies occur of roles for the self or others, and the patients have drifting, possibly dramatic lives with a feeling that reality is not really real and the self is not in control or responsible.

Medium-order patterns are related to attention-seeking behavior, childlike qualities, passivity or infirmity, fluid change in mood and emotion, lability, etc.

Short-order patterns affect the information-processing style and include global deployment of attention, vague and incomplete communication of ideas and feelings, and non-verbal communications not always translated into conscious meaning. They occur with only partial or unidirectional lines of association and with a tendency to shortcircuit problematic thoughts to an apparent completion.

These descriptions probably need more detail and explanation to be readily accepted as evidence of definable phenomena. However they constitute a move towards grouping phenomena which are felt to be common with the hysterical personality. It is reasonable to hope that in due course they will be better elucidated and put into an appropriate form for testing.

A further valuable discussion of the hysterical personality is provided by Blacker and Tupin (Blacker and Tupin, 1977) who argue that the core descriptors of the hysterical personality are aggressive behavior, emotionality, sexual problems, obstinacy, exhibitionism, egocentricity, and sexual provocativeness and dependency. These will appear either with a pseudofeminine or pseudomasculine expression and such patterns can be described and characterized. The dynamics postulated to account for the personality features in the more severe cases are that there is an infantile personality organization as a result of inadequate mothering and deprivation in infancy which results in extreme and unstable behavior as an adult. The less severely damaged—more mature—hysterical personality has experienced less early deprivation and more success at school, work and socially. The central issue for the individual in either type is held to be the resolution of gender identity shown by the types of behavior described above which are characteristic of the hysterical personality.

Cultural and Organic Influences

The fundamental topics of the dissociative symptoms and of the hysterical personality have been briefly outlined.

There is also an enormous and fascinating variety of physical and cultural factors which promote hysterical complaints. In numerous cultures instances have been described of the mass induction of hysterical symptoms. Merskey (Merskey 1979a) gives an account of some of these cases which were first described extensively by Hecker (Hecker, 1844). Medieval populations in Europe, nuns in the 18th century, school children, factory workers and nurses have all provided examples of the epidemic spread of hysterical symptoms. In medieval Italy (and the modern world?) continuous dancing or tarantism was one manifestation; more often today epidemic fainting and nausea occur. As mentioned earlier there is reason to believe that the traditional hysterical symptoms have declined in the more developed world. Whilst classical conversion such as astasia-abasia, paralysis, fits and anastias still occur relatively readily in unsophisticated populations (Lambo, 1956; Kagua, 1964; Chang and Kim, 1973; Armstrong and Patterson, 1975) they are relatively infrequent in urban centers, except in certain settings such as neurological clinics as mentioned above. Complaints of headache or back pain seem to serve an hysterical function in the more sophisticated groups. Abse (Abse, 1966) showed how the prognosis of hysteria was more often marked by the classical motor symptoms in Indian soldiers and by headache in British ones, and there is considerable evidence that pain, especially chronic pain, is utilized as a hysterical symptom (Merskey, 1979a, 1979b).

It is only possible here to hint at the variety and interest of the ways in which culture and experience promote the patterns of hysterical symptoms. But any observer of society and of medical practice will notice a few.

A more difficult question has to do with the relationship of organic brain disease to hysterical symptoms. It is easy to comprehend that patients with existing illness under stress might replicate symptoms they saw or experienced in the past, or enlarge upon symptoms from which they currently suffer. However many authors, reviewed by Guttman (Guttman, 1932), have noted a high association between some cerebral lesions and hysteria, and between epilepsy and hysteria. Credner (Credner, 1930) found 73 of 200 patients with hysterical symptoms had frontal lesions. Schilder (Schilder, 1935, 1939, 1940) suggested that the cerebral lesions contributed in some special way to the development of the hysterical symptom. This idea has been received sympathetically by later authors (Slater, 1965; Whitlock, 1967; Merskey and Buhrich, 1975) who all seemed to feel that the change of brain function predisposes to the emergence of hysterical symptoms. The simplest idea, which is put forward by Slater, is that the lesion promotes regression of the personality. Ludwig (Ludwig, 1972) makes a brave attempt at a more direct conceptual hypothesis involving "selective depression of awareness of a bodily function" but this can only be very speculative at the present time.

More importantly, we can recognize that in medical practice lately, the commonest place of presentation of classical hysterical symptoms is the neurological clinic. The main or only exceptions are in unsophisticated populations as already outlined, and in certain situations where compensation is involved.

This means that while the principal explanation of hysterical symptoms remains dynamic in nature we have also to accept that cerebral lesions or dysfunction have a special tendency to cause hysterical symptoms and the way in which this occurs may well turn out to be of theoretical and practical importance.

DIAGNOSIS AND TREATMENT

As indicated earlier, if a specialist is to make the diagnosis of classical hysterical symptoms it is usually best done by a neurologist. His skills in examination are the most relevant. Confirmation of the presence of a relevant conflict and of the significance of the personality and its problems are best provided by the psychiatrist. In practice it seems that from the psychiatric aspect most hysterical symptoms occur in one or another context from the following list (Merskey, 1975a) which was originally suggested by Dr. R. T. C. Pratt in a personal communication:

1. Hysteria with one or two symptoms, usually motor or dissociative (as in amnesia), sometimes pain

2. Polysymptomatic hysteria, especially hypochondriasis and Briquet's syndrome

3. Hysterical elaboration or organic complaints

4. Symptoms of self-induced illness or self-damage in abnormal personalities ranging from anorexia nervosa to hospital addiction

5. Psychotic or pseudopsychotic disorders (Ganser's syndrome, hysterical psychosis)

6. Hysterical personality

7. Culturally sanctioned endemic or epidemic hysteria

The prognosis in these cases depends upon the context. Monosymptomatic complaints and epidemic attacks have the best prognosis. The former recover in as many as 90 percent or more of cases initially and 70 percent stay well for four to six years (Carter, 1949). Less acute monosymptomatic cases do not do quite so well and in a series of 98 patients followed by Lewis (Lewis, 1975) approximately 60 percent were well or consistently better after at least seven years. Seven patients had died (three of probably nervous system disorders, one by suicide). Ciompi (Ciompi, 1969) who examined 38 patients who had survived an average of 34 years found that 20 percent were chronically affected. Hysterical personality patterns showed less change for the better. At the other end of the scale, Briquet's syndrome can be expected only to improve in minor respects.

Treatment has to be guided by these observations as well as by knowledge of potential causes. In one sense it is not different from much of the rest of psychiatry. The relevant characteristics and experiences of the patient are determined and the attempt is made to form a relationship which will prove helpful in working with the patient. Potential conflicts are sought and efforts are made to resolve them either by a change in the patient's circumstances, or by a change in his feelings, attitudes and methods of adjustment. This is undertaken on the basis of anything from a single interview to prolonged psychotherapy, depending upon the case.

Unlike the common practice in some other areas of psychiatry, drug treatment, except as a placebo, is normally avoided. More particularly, the physician has to be aware of his own reactions to the possibility that he is being manipulated. Besides the transference—or special feeling—which the patient may initially develop for the physician, there is also an increased likelihood with hysterical complaints of a negative counter-tranference appearing. That is to say the physician develops feelings of uneasiness or anger in respect of the patient. The best prophylactic against this hazard is continual vigilance in regard to one's own feelings. It is essential to feel sympathy for the patient if good results are to be obtained, but the sympathy must be restrained and tolerance is *de rigeur.*

Of course many types of enthusiastic treatment have also been successful varying from hypnosis to behavior therapy. The former is often no more that a maneuver which like many others provides a face-saving opportunity to lose a symptom. Successes reported for the latter may also be regarded "as providing the patient with an adequately impressive 'excuse to get better' " (Bird, 1979). In all these circumstances it is important to note that if the symptom is removed and a significant underlying conflict is left unresolved, the patient may become seriously depressed and even suicidal. This is not a common occurrence and symptom substitution of this sort may appear only in a minority of patients but it does sometimes happen. The direct removal of a hysterical symptom by suggestion, hypnosis or behavior therapy, should therefore only be practiced when the patient is assured of continuing support and assistance with dilemmas which re-appear.

Provided the physician is willing to ensure this precaution, and is able to convey to the patient the assurance that his help will remain available, he may embark with confidence upon the interesting and generally rewarding task of treating hysterical symptoms. In doing so, he should beware of one other hazard. It often works very badly to take an immediate direct approach and to say "something unconscious is upsetting you." The frequent reply is "I have told you everything." It is usually more successful to speak perfectly truthfully of ways in which the emotions may influence the body and then discursively approach any topics which are likely to be a source of the trouble. If this is done it is much easier to remove the symptom (if necessary, by some placebo technique) after the main emotional obstacles have been tackled. However, if an emotional problem cannot be uncovered, then some technique which removes the symptom first may be employed, to be succeeded by discussion or psychotherapy or other help which deals with the problems uncovered.

REFERENCES

Abse, D. W. *Hysteria and Related Mental Disroders.* Wright, Bristol (1966).

Alexander, F. *Fundamentals of Psychoanalysis.* Norton and Co., New York (1963).

Armstong, H. and Patterson, P. Seizures in Canadian Indian children. *Canad. Psychiat. Ass. J.* 20,247-255 (1975).

Blacker, K. H. and Tupin, J. P. Hysteria and Hysterical Structures: Developmental and Social Theories in *Hysterical Personality.* Horowitz, M. J., ed. Jason Aronson, New York (1977).

Briquet, P. *Traite Clinique et Therapetuique de l'Hysterie.* J. B. Bailliere & Fils, Paris (1859).

Carter, A. B. The prognosis of certain hysterical symptoms. *Brit Med. J.* 1, 1076-1079 (1949).

Chang, S. K. and Kim, K. I. Psychiatry in South Korea. *Amer. J. Psychiat.* 130, 667-669 (1973).

Charcot, J. M. *Clinical Lectures on Diseases of the Nervous System* Savill, T., trans. New Sydenham Soc., vol 3 London (1889).

Chertok, L "Hysteria" versus "Briquet's Syndrome". *Amer. J. Psychiat.* 132, 1087 (1975).

Chodoff, P. and Lyons, H. Hysteria, the hysterical personality and 'hysterical' conversion. *Amer. J. Psychiat.* 114, 734-740 (1958).

Ciompi, L. Follow-up studies on the evolution of former neurotic and depressive states in old age. Clinical and psychodynamic aspects. *J.Geriat. Psychiat.* 3, 90-106 (1969).

Cloninger, C. R. and Guze, S. B. Female criminals: Their personal, familial and social backgrounds. The relation of these to the diagnoses of sociopathy and hysteria. *Arch. Gen. Psychiat.* 23, 554-558 (1970).

Credner, L. Klinische und soziale Auswirkungen von Hirnschadigungen. *Zeitschr. f. d. ges. Neurol. u. Psychiat.* 126, 721-757 (1930).

De Alarcon, R. Hysteria and hysterical personality: How come one without the other? *Psychiat. Q.* 47, 258-275 (1973).

Freud, S. (1893-1895), Breuer, J. E. and Freud, S. 1955. *Studies in Hysteria. Complete Psychological Works. Standard Ed.,* vol. 2, Hogarth Press.

Gowers, W. R. *A Manual of Diseases of the Nervous System,* 1 & 2. J. & A. Churchill, London (1893).

Guttman, E. Organische Krankheitsbilder hysterischen Geprages. *Fortschr. Neurol Psychiat.* 4,82-99 (1932).

Guze, S. B. The Role of Follow-up Studies: Their Contribution to Diagnostic Classification As Applied to Hysteria. *Seminars in Psychiat.* 2,392-402 (1970).

Hecker, J. F. C. *Epidemics of the Middle Ages* Babington, B. G., trans. New Sydenham Soc., London (1844).

Hirsch, J. J. and Hollender, M. H. Hysterical psychosis. Clarification of the concept. *Amer. J. Psychiat.* 125,909-915 (1969).

Horowitz, M. J. The Core Characteristics of Hysterical Personality, in *Hysterical Personality,* Horowitz, M. J., ed. Jason Aronson, New York (1977).

Janet, P. *L'Etat Mental des Hysteriques.* Rueff, Paris (1894).

Kagwa, B. H. The problem of mass hysteria in East Africa. *E. Afr. Med. J.* 41,560-566 (1964).

Kraepelin, E. Lectures on Clinical Psychiatry, Lecture XXVI on Hysterical Insanity, Johnstone, T., trans. William Wood and Co, New York (1904).

Lambo, T. A. Neuropsychiatric problems in Nigeria. *Brit. Med. J.* 2, 1388-1394 (1956).

Lazare, A. The hysterical character in psychoanalytic theory. *Arch. Gen. Psychiat.* 25, 131-137 (1971).

Lewis, A. J. Psychological Medicine, in *A Textbook of the Practice of Medicine,* 8th ed, Price, F. S., ed. Oxford Medical Publications, London (1950).

Lewis, A. J. The survival of hysteria. *Psychol. Med.* 5,9-12 (1975).

Ljungberg, L. Hysteria. *Acta Psychiat., Scand. Suppl.* 112 (1957).

Ludwig, A. M. Hysteria - a neurobiological theory. *Arch. Gen. Psychiat.* 27,771-777 (1972).

Mai, F. M. and Merskey, H. The Treatise on Hysteria of P. Briquet: a synopsis and commentary. (1979) Submitted for publication.

Marmor, J. Orality in the hysterical personality. *J. Amer. Psychoanal. Assoc.* 1,656-671 (1953).

Merskey, H. Psychological aspects of pain. *Postgrad. Med. J.* 44,297-306 (1968).

Merskey, H. *The Analysis of Hysteria.* Baillere Tindall, London (1979a).

Merskey, H. Psychological and Psychiatric Aspects of Pain Control, in *Pain: Meaning and Management.* Smith, W. L., Merskey, H., and Gross, S. C., ed. Spectrum Publications (1979b).

Merskey, H. and Buhrich, N. A. Hysteria and organic brain disease. *Brit. J. Med. Psychol.* 48,359-366 (1975).

Merskey, H. and Trimble, M. Personality, sexual adjustment and brain lesions in patients with conversion symptoms. *Amer. J. Psychiat.* 136,2,179-182 (1979).

Miller, N. E. Applications of Learning and Biofeedback to Psychiatry, in *Comprehensive Textbook of Psychiatry,* 2nd Ed., Freedman, A. M., Kaplan, H. I., and Sadock, B. J., ed. Williams and Wilkins, Baltimore (1974).

Schilder, P. 1935. *The Image and Appearance of the Human Body.* Internat. Universities Press (1951).

Schilder, P. The concept of hysteria. *Amer. J. Psychiat.* 95,1389-1413 (1939).

Schilder, P. Neurosis Following Head and Brain Injuries, in *Injuries of the Skull, Brain and Spinal Cord.* Brock, S., ed. Williams and Wilkins, Philadelphia (1940).

Shapiro, D. *Neurotic Sytles.* Basic Books, New York (1965).

Slater, E. Diagnosis of "Hysteria". *Brit. Med. J.* 1,1395-1399 (1965).

Whitlock, F. A. The Aetiology of Hysteria. *Acta Psychiat. Scand.* 43,144-162 (1967).

Woodruff, R. A. Jr. Hysteria: An evaluation of objective diagnostic criteria by the study of women with chronic medical illnesses. *Brit. J. Psychiat.* 114,1115-1119 (1968).

8
Conversion Disorders:
A Challenge to Medicine

RICHARD W. REWEY

INTRODUCTION

Physicians through the centuries have been challenged with the need of diagnosing and treating conversion disorders in their patients. The latter term is the modern equivalent of *hystera*, the Greek word for uterus, anglicized to hysteria. The Greeks felt these disorders were exclusively of women and were due to abnormal movements of the uterus. This concept of uterine etiology for many emotional problems in women, although long since proven erroneous in most cases, still has its present-day adherents in the medical community and may account for some of the unnecessary hysterectomies that we see.

In the Middle Ages, hysterical clinical syndromes were recognized and described, but the women so afflicted were believed to be witches demonically possessed. By the 1600's, with the return of interest in scientific medicine, Thomas Sydenham recognized that hysterical phenomena had no true physical pathology, although they could mimic most known physical diseases (Freedman and Kaplan, 1967).

The psychogenic etiology of conversion phenomena did not become seriously espoused until the arrival of Sigmund Freud and his contemporaries in the late 1800's. Charcot, a neurologst, reintroduced hypnotism and, through the use of posthypnotic suggestion, showed that hysterical symptoms could be induced and removed in these very suggestible patients. Charcot, however, felt that the conversion phenomenon was fundamentally a neurological disorder. It remained for Janet to introduce the

concept of *dissociation* of consciousness (Janet, 1907) to account for the origin of hysterical symptoms and
dissociative states, including amnesias, somnambulisms,
fugues and multiple personalities. Freud refined Janet's
formulation and added the concepts of *repression* of painful
affects and ideas out of conscious awareness, and the *conversion* of these into somatic hysterical symptoms which
symbolically represented some earlier life trauma (Freud,
1962). Thus, these sequential and interlocking conceptual
mechanisms of repression, dissociation, and conversion offered the early psychoanalysts a comprehensive and effective basis for understanding and treating conversion
phenomena as a mental disorder. During Freud's time, the
term hysteria became known as conversion hysteria,
which in turn became known as conversion reaction
following World War II. At that time, conversion reaction
was defined by the American Psychiatric Association as "a
syndrome in which impulses causing anxiety are con-
verted into one or more functional symptoms in organs or
parts of the body, usually those that are under voluntary
control. The symptoms serve to lessen conscious anxiety
and usually are symbolic of underlying mental conflict
(*Standard Nomenclature,*)." With the arrival of the
American Psychiatric Association's Diagnostic and
Statistical Manual of Mental Disorders of 1980 (DSM--III),
the term conversion reaction is replaced by *conversion
disorder,* which will be the definitive term used throughout
the rest of this paper. Conversion disorder is now defined
as "a clinical picture in which the predominant disturbance is a loss of or alteration in physical functioning that
suggests physical disorder but which instead is apparently
an expression of psychological conflict or need. The disturbance is not under voluntary control, and after appropriate
investigation cannot be explained by any physical disorder
or known pathophysiological mechanism (*Diagnostic and
Statistical Manual,* 1980).

Freud conceptualized conversion hysteria as a specific
clinical entity arising from specific sexual conflicts
originating in early development, precipitated in adult life
conflicts over the sex drive, and perpetuated by secondary

gain (Freud, 1962). This dynamic explanation may be the correct basis for many conversion disorders, though does by no means appear to account satisfactorily for all disorders that are now recognized. For instance, in wartime the development of conversion disorders appears to follow a case of combat neurosis with the more obvious motivation being survival rather than the resolution of some sexual conflict. Conversion phenomena also develop in patients with personality disorders as an apparent means of having dependency needs gratified. Although Frued described the disorder initially in hysterical neurotics, we have become aware over the past several decades that conversion symptoms may accompany various classes of psychopathology; they can occur in other psychoneuroses and also transiently in the personality disorders and the schizophrenias (Freedman and Kaplan, 1967).

Finally, I will make brief mention here of the differentiation of conversion symptoms from psychosomatic ones. Primarily, conversion phenomena are mediated through the voluntary nervous system rather than the autonomic or involuntary nervous system as in psychosomatic symptoms. Secondly, conversion symptoms tend to be more limited in terms of bondaries, these usually corresponding to the patient's idea of how his or her disability should be manifested, rather that utilizing a true CNS pathway impairment. The latter could produce psychosomatic afflictions when the involuntary or autonomic system is involved and localizing neurologically diagnosable lesions when the voluntary nervous system is involved. Thus, the basic difference is that conversion disorder is primarily a mental disorder which would appear to involve neurological impairment at first glance, whereas psychosomatic symptoms and diseases actually do involve abnormal pathway functioning and end organ response with eventual end organ damage if chronic or untreated (Freedman and Kaplan, 1967). Although the psychosomatic conditions quite clearly have stress as an etiological factor of varying importance, it is well to keep in mind that such patients should be considered to have true physiological dysfunction, probably of complex multifactorial etiology, including constitutional predisposition. Psychotherapy often is of only partial benefit for such patients, and our treatment approach must be more broadly based, including thorough medical followthrough, especially in light of the natural history of end organ damage in many of these conditions. Conversely, conversion disorder is a mental disorder in which mental mechanisms unconsciously select the area of symptomatology and in which area no abnormal physiology is to be found, nor really need be looked for exhaustively beyond the characteristic findings in physical examination mentioned elsewhere in this book. Therefore, as I will again mention later, the diagnosis of conversion disorder should be made affirmatively rather than by exclusion, should be made on a history of emotional conflict temporally relevant to the onset of symptoms, and by characteristic findings on physical examination. Although this distinction between conversion and psychosomatic symptoms may sometimes be difficult and complicated by the fact that both types of problems can occur in the same patient, if the above differentiating factors are firmly kept in mind and adhered to, the primary physician will be able to make these differentiations quite accurately in most cases. He can then direct his, or the consulting psychiatrist's, attention to those symptoms which more clearly fit the conversion definition and therefore should be more amenable to psychotherapeutic intervention in a sufficiently motivated patient. Psychiatric attention should also be given to many patients with psychosomatic conditions, though these conditions will require a correspondingly different approach and level of expectation of change as well as a somewhat more retrictive role for the mental health professional than will conversion symptoms.

CLINICAL DESCRIPTION

Although conversion phenomena appear to be more frequent in women, the incidence in men is certainly significant and may actually be equal in some conditions, especially when compensation is an issue. Conversion disorder can appear at any time from early adolescence on through the later decades of life, though they appear most frequently in adolescence or early adulthood. The manifestations may be sporadic and episodic, often arising at times of emotional stress resulting from external crises. The location and type of symptoms may be extremely variable even within the same person and may change quite rapidly, or single symptoms may persist for years (Freedman and Kaplan, 1967).

Although the possible manifestations of conversion disorder are almost beyond number and may mimic any known bodily disease, they can usually be classified in four major categories: the motor disturbances, sensory disturbances, conversion symptoms simulating physical illness and those complicating physical illness (Freedman and Kaplan, 1967). The motor disturbances include many possible forms, including rhythmical tremors, choreiform ticks and jerks and hysterical pseudoseizures. All of these are more likely to be exhibited when the patient is being observed and frequently will not be present when the patient thinks he is not being observed. Hysterical pseudoseizures usually are quite dramatic; the patient will appear wild and disorganized and totally out of control but will rarely hurt himself. When pseudoseizures occur with other conversion phenomena such as tunnel vision, visual hallucinations or hysterial hemiplegia, the diagnosis is made somewhat easier. Perhaps the most difficult patient to diagnose having pseudoseizure activity is that patient who does have true neurogenic seizures, and who because of emotional stress and personality instability will develop concommitant pseudoseizures as well. Such patients present very complicated management problems and are usually best approached by a psychiatrist working in close cooperation with the neurologist, internist, or other physician treating the neurogenic seizures. Paralysis or paresis may be seen, usually affecting the extremities, and may present as a monoplegia, hemiplegia, or paraplegia but rarely a total quadraplegia. The usual differentiating features in history and physical examination mentioned elsewhere in this volume will be found in these patients, and they should be referred for psychiatric attention as soon as the diagnosis is conclusively made.

A particularly interesting form of movement disorder is hysterical aphonia, in which the patient claims to be unable to talk but in fact can usually whisper and can make all of the normal movements of the muscles of phonation. One such interesting patient was a university graduate student who felt ill-prepared for his upcoming oral and written examinations and developed a case of hysterial aphonia in conjunction with a dissociative fugue state on the eve of his examinations! This patient was admitted to the psychiatric unit and communicated exclusively by handwriting for the next ten days. From the beginning, he was given considerable reassurance that in fact he had suffered no injury of his vocal chords or the like and that as soon as he felt less emotionally stressed, his speech would return. This reassurance, along with supportive psychotherapy and appropriate medication for anxiety, resulted in a fairly rapid recovery with partial return of his speech in ten days and full return of speech by fourteen days after the onset of his condition. Interestingly, he spent most of his free time on the psychiatric unit studying intensively for the examinations he had not been able to take. He was given some tutorial assistance and allowed liberal visiting hours with fellow students to assist him in his exam preparation. He took his examinations and passed them successfully within a few days after return of his speech and his subsequent discharge. Clearly, the return of his speech occurred around the time he felt ready to take his tests. His hysterical aphonia relieved him of the need of taking his oral examinations, which had to be taken at the same time as the written examinations, and hence the aphonia was his way of dissociating this entire stressful challenge from his life temporarily.

A variety of sensory disturbances can occur in conversion disorders. When these involve the limbs, there is usually a general sensory inpairment of all modalities along with paralysis or paresis of the involved area. The classical stocking or glove pattern, which represents the patient's concept of impairment, is often seen here. These straight lines of demarcation between normal and impaired sensation are also seen when the area of involvement affects the midline of the body, whereas a true neural lesion will show spreading across the midline. A conversion disorder involving a special sense organ, including sight, hearing and taste, can also be involved, and features differentiating these in conversion versus neurogenic syndromes are well known and described in the literature. Suffice it to say that these disturbances tend to be inconstant and that through a variety of close observation and clinical maneuvers, accurate differentiation can be made. Hallucinations occur frequently in hysterical patients and these are most commonly visual in nature. They tend to be quite stereotyped, frequently the same hallucination occurring repeatedly and quite vividly, as described by the patient. Visual hallucinations are usually hysterical, with the exceptions of toxic delerium, drug side effects, or psychomotor seizures.

Hysterical pain, now referred to as Psychogenic Pain Disorder in the DSM--III (*Diagnostic and Statistical Manual, 1980*) seems to be very common and perhaps is becoming even more common in our society. The pain is vaguely described, tends to be intermittent, and frequently is inconsistently localized. When pressed for specific description, the patients are often unable to give a consistent description of the characteristics of the pain, in contrast to the pain from an organic origin which tends to be more consistently described. Though the most common site of hysterical pain is the abdomen, especially in women, the number of psychogenic pain patients presenting with chronic low back pain seems to be on the increase, especially among men. These patients do not show the classical *la belle indifference* of most conversion patients; on the contrary they are usually demanding of medicaion or corrective surgery, and seem to be particularly resistive to accepting psychogenic interpretation of their problem. Some of these patients merge into another group in which conversion symptoms appear to be complicating or protracting a physical illness, such as the example given previously of hysterical seizures complicating true neurogenic seizures.

Many patients with hysterical pain had a previous organic lesion in the area of the pain or some other area in their body, which, even though physically healed, seems to provide a foundation for the development of subsequent functional or psychogenic pain. The concept of somatic compliance (Freedman and Kaplan, 1967) is exemplified very nicely here, in which conversion symptoms tend to appear in locations and organ systems that are or have previously been the site of symptom-producing lesions. Finally, there are patients in whom conversion symptoms stimulate a physical illness, the latter often occurring in a person with whom the hysterical patient has a close relationship (Freud, 1962). This kind of reaction is frequently seen as part of a pathological grief reaction in which the conversion patient has lost a close significant other from some illness or injury, and then develops that same afflication himself in symbolic representation through the means of a conversion disorder. Certainly the defense of identification with the significant other is at work here, along with an unwillingness or difficulty in letting go of a deceased loved one. The therapeutic challenge to the psychiatrist is to help the person through their grief reaction so that they can recompensate their own bodily integrity and separate from the departed siginificant other. Efforts made toward symptom removal as an initial approach in such patients are usually bound to fail, and even if successful, will run the risk of exacerbating the grieving process.

BEHAVIORAL CHARACTERISTICS
OF CONVERSION DISORDER PATIENTS

The most common behavioral feature in conversion patients is *la belle indifference,* which is defined as the total unconcern about their disturbance and function, so much so that the patient may not even mention the symptom to the doctor, thus producing a crucial error of omission in the medical workup. *La belle indifference* needs to be differentiated from hypochondriasis, in which the person has an exaggerated concern about symptoms. *La belle indifference* in the classical sense, although usually present in some degree in true conversion, is not always present, and it would seem that we probably have a continuum in the degree of expressed concern from total unconcern all the way out to high degrees of concern about a particular symptom. This is probably best explainable on the basis of great individual differences in the degree of repression, dissociation, and conversion defenses utilized in the origin and continuation of the disorder.

Although conversion disorder can occur in major mental illness such as schizophrenia, the fact is that most conversion patients show little if any major abnormality in their mental status examination and will usually show no features of psychosis or organic brain dysfunction. Frequently some or all of the features of true hysterical personality will be found. These include dramatic tendencies in movement and language. Such patients have been described as talking more about the effect of symptoms on their life rather than the symptoms themselves (Freedman and Kaplan, 1967). They are often histrionic, exhibitionistic, narcissistic, seductive, very dependent, and manipulative of others to meet their dependency needs and perpetuate the secondary gain from their impairment. They give the distinct impression of using their symptoms to extract care and concern from family, friends, and most of all from doctors. Yet a puzzling ambivalence, if not *la belle indifference*, about the actual symptoms themselves will be seen, with the end result often being that in spite of much strong manipulation and demands for relief, they will not follow through with prescribed treatment and will sometimes present an almost tempting challenge to the doctor to "see if you can make my problem go away." Such messages tend to reinforce the prevailing wisdom in medicine and psychiatry that, for a period of time at least, conversion disorder patients often seem to need their symptoms, and will actually sabotage premature efforts directed toward symptom removal before their basic emotional conflicts are dealt with adequately. Finally, the patient with borderline personality disorder will frequently present with conversion symptoms and will present a doubly difficult challenge to the psychiatrist or other physician involved. In addition to all of the above personality features frequently seen, these patients engage in splitting (alternately vilifying and then deifying various people

DIAGNOSIS OF CONVERSION DISORDER

including doctors) and brief episodes of paranoid thinking, frequently in response to unexpected or unwelcome statements from the doctor. In addition, there and other patients with conversion disorder are prone to impulsive acting–out behavior including suicidal gestures such as overdoses or wrist slashing. Thus, these patients call for tremendous reassurance and support, but also firm consistency from those of us who dare to treat them.

As mentioned previously, the diagnosis should be made on an affirmative basis through appropriate history and positive findings on physical examination including thorough mental status and neurological examinations. It should not be a diagnosis made by excluion, which is usually characterized as an exhaustive, extensive attempt to eliminate all possible or likely afflictions in the involved area through the use of highly specialized tests and x-rays. The possible conversion disorder patient must be allowed to tell his own history, and the physician ought not be too directive or judgmental-sounding in taking the history. As in most other conditions in medicine, when we allow the patient to tell his own story, it is surprising how frequently the pathology or psychopathology can really quite accurately be inferred even before a physical examination or specialized testing is undertaken. The possibility of some true organic pathology in a patient who also has some conversion symptoms must of course constantly be considered, and above all we must not commit the cardinal sin of categorizing people as totally functional versus organic when considering what is wrong with them.

The diagnosis of conversion disorder is suggested by one or all of the following factors (Freedman and Kaplan, 1967). 1. A history of other symptoms past or concurrent that have clear characteristics of conversion disorder. 2. Somatic compliance. 3. History of other overtly neurotic symptoms. 4. A past hisotry of complex or multiple illnesses for which no clear-cut physical origin was ever found and which may have resulted in unnecessary surgery. 5. A history of sexual disturbances. 6. Hysterical personality behavioral characteristics. 7. *La belle indif-*

ference. 8. The recent death of a person important to the patient or other disturbances in personal relationships temporally related to the onset of symptoms. 9. Differential findings on physicial examination already mentioned. 10. Response to attempts at symptom removal under hypnosis or sodium anytal interview.

Psychological or neuropsychological testing may be very useful in offering confirmatory or localizing observations regarding the patient's psychopathology detected in clinical mental status examination. The latter may be quite insufficient, though, in shedding accurate light on a person's full personality mechanisms, and these are often more sharply elucidated through the testing medium. The results of these tests should be thought of as useful adjuvants in assessing personality and mental status, but should not be thought of as offering a definitive answer about whether or not a particular symptom is functional or organic.

PROGNOSIS AND TREATMENT

It has been noted by several authors that the prognosis of conversion disorder really has little to do with the degree of functional impairment of the actual symptomatology, but rather more specifically rests on the degree of psychological disturbance underlying the outward symptomatology (Freud, 1962). As a rule, the more disturbed the personality, the more multiple symptoms will be presented and the more chronic the conversion disorder will be. Many of the very chronic multiple symptom patients are classified as Briquet's syndrome or Somatoform disorder and are truly multiple problem patients with a frequent tendency toward chronicity.

Treatment considerations of the conversion patient frequently need to involve several approaches simultaneously, including psychotherapy, appropriate medication, environmental manipulation, etc. Certainly psychotherapy is indicated for most conversion patients, although it is distressing how often the patient will reject this recommendation even if the therapy can be offered by a nonphysician, who is usually seen as less threatening than a

physician, particularly a psychiatrist. If a therapeutic relationship with a mental health professional can be formed,
however, this is generally felt to be a favorable prognostic
sign and the patient can then have individual, marital,
family, or group therapy alone or in combination as the
primary treatment approach. As mentioned, these patients
need tremendous amounts of support and reassurance
along with the specific suggestion, as in the case of the
university student with hysterical aphonia, that their
disabling symptoms will improve and that they have no
serious bodily disease. Psychotropic medications can be
useful for treating specific psychiatric symptomatology
which may be found in the conversion patient, though no
specific psychotropic medication is indicated for conversion disorder in the general sense. Many of these people
are chronically anxious and unable to relax, so that the use
of relaxation training, hypnosis, or meditation in addition
to psychotherapy can be useful adjuvants; but regarding
the use of hypnosis we need to be very careful not to "take
away" the patient's symptoms too quickly lest we see
symptom substitution or even further regression than we
had before the attempted symptom removal. It is necessary to take a supportive and reassuring, though not overly
solicitous, attitude with a conversion patient. We must
walk a narrow line between providing a trusting therapeutic relationship versus encouraging further regression and
psychological invalidism. Generally speaking, the less
focus in therapy on the particular symptom the more likely
it is it remit more quickly. In other words, the less the
symptom is reinforced either positively or negatively, the
less secondary gain is acquired by the patient and the more
he will be able to direct his attention toward his strengths
and needs for growth in the psychotherapy rehabilitation
process. Finally, the use of environmental manipulation
has long been an obvious and helpful assist in treating the
conversion patient. In this sense, hospitalization in effect
was a temporary means of environmental manipulation for
the university graduate student with hysterical aphonia,
and had the effect of removing him from his stressful
pre-examination environment. This manipulation also

provided him a safe, reassuring refuge while his regressive tendencies could be countered and his growth-oriented and success-directed efforts could go forward more effectively. I have found it useful with these patients to project some arbitrary, though realistic, time limit during which I expect to work with them fairly intensively, and by the end of which time I expect them to have been able to regain most of their lost function. This is a particularly useful approach to take when the patient has a truly debilitating symptom preventing him from going forward in the major direction in his life, again the example of the graduate student being a good one in that regard. This of course assumes that the basic precipitating crises which provoked the conversion disorder can be dealt with successfully during that time, and it is surprising how frequently this can be done. Certainly the good outcomes of military physicians in aggressively treating battle field conversion disorders and dissociative states during and since World War II, emphasizing only short-term interruption from the soldier's front line duty, has more than been borne out in comparable civilian experience in the practice of medicine in this country and other countries since then.

In conclusion, conversion disorders present us with problems which seem initially to be perplexing and very frustrating, but which if properly diagnosed and approached from a scientific basis, can not only show fairly rapid remission but also can have the effect of fostering the patient's confidence in the doctor's ability to help him. This can allow the treatment relationship to progress on to more basic, though less outwardly obvious, problems in the person's life.

REFERENCES

Diagnostic and Statistical Manual of Mental Disorders, Third Edition, American Psychiatric Association, p. 244 (1980).

Freedman, A. and Kaplan, H. Comprehensive Textbook of Psychiatry. Williams & Wilkins Co., Baltimore, p. 871 (1967).

Freud, S. *Standard Edition of the Complete Works of Sigmund Freud.* Hogarth Press, London (1962).

Janet, P. *The Major Symptoms of Hysteria.* Macmillan, New York (1907).

Standard Nomenclature of Diseases and Operations, American Psychiatric Association.

Index